This book belongs to:
George Parry 3/27/65

ARNOLD PALMER

My Game
and
Yours

SIMON AND SCHUSTER   NEW YORK

FIRST PRINTING

DESIGNED BY EVE METZ

LIBRARY OF CONGRESS CATALOG CARD NUMBER: 65–15025

MANUFACTURED IN THE UNITED STATES OF AMERICA

COLOR BY RAINBOW LITHOGRAPHERS, NEW YORK

TEXT AND BINDING BY AMERICAN BOOK–STRATFORD PRESS, NEW YORK

TO MY WIFE, WINNIE

CONTENTS

CONTENTS

CHAPTER I

GOLF IS EASIER
THAN YOU THINK

GOLF IS DECEPTIVELY SIMPLE and endlessly complicated. A child can play it well and a grown man can never master it. Any single round of it is full of unexpected triumphs and perfect shots that end in disaster. It is almost a science, yet it is a puzzle without an answer. It is gratifying and tantalizing, precise and unpredictable; it requires complete concentration and total relaxation. It satisfies the soul and frustrates the intellect. It is at the same time rewarding and maddening—and it is without doubt the greatest game mankind has ever invented.

One strange trouble that plagues me, as a professional who has to keep winning to keep eating, is that I love the game so much that I sometimes forget to play it as well as I can. Especially in the spring of the year, when the first warm sun presses down on your shoulders, when the grass has just been mowed for the first time and sits there damp and green, with its fresh-cut smell floating up to your nostrils, when the sky is a deep blue roof over your head and an occasional cloud drifts by so white that it dazzles your eyes, a golf course is an intoxicating place.

This was the sort of day, this was the sort of happiness, that we kept waiting for all winter when I was growing up in western Pennsylvania. The winters are long and hard around Latrobe, my home town; the golf course where my father was and is the pro usually was frozen over from the middle of December; we had to content ourselves with skiing until that first perfect day came along some time toward the end of March. We dreamed about it all winter and went slightly out of our minds when it finally arrived.

I still have trouble keeping my feet on the ground on that kind of day; I want to march right up over the next hill and on and on into the heavens. Life is so wonderful; it is so great to be alive and playing golf; the world is so perfect that my mind sloshes around aimlessly like a baby enjoying a bath. I forget that the ball is there to be hit. I stare at it, its white enamel nesting in the grass, as if hypnotized. Physically I am on the golf course but spiritually I am somewhere else, somewhere out in that wild blue yonder, and I have to make a deliberate effort to reach out, pull myself back and get down to business.

What other people may find in poetry or art museums, I find in the flight of a good drive—the white ball sailing up and up into that blue sky, growing smaller and smaller, almost taking off in orbit, then suddenly reaching its apex, curving, falling, describing the perfect parabola of a good hit, and finally dropping to the turf to roll some more, the way I planned it. I even enjoy the mingled pleasure and discomfort of breaking in a new pair of golf shoes. I like the firmness of the leather, the solid feeling against the turf. Sometimes I have changed to a new pair of shoes in the middle of a tournament, have been carried away by the confidence they gave me and the excitement of the play, and have not noticed until I returned to the clubhouse that I had acquired a crop of blisters.

Sometimes, however, I get dead tired of golf. One tournament has followed another, day in and day out. I am mentally and physically exhausted. My back aches from the constant turning, shot after shot. My shoulders hurt from the constant jar of clubhead biting into hard earth. I cannot wait to get back home, to toss the clubs into a dark closet, to sit down, relax and forget there ever was such a game. I sit for an entire day and no thought of golf ever enters my head. The second morning also passes in blissful freedom from the tyranny of the game. But, by the second afternoon, I am downstairs in my shop, fiddling with that 3-wood that felt a little off-balance in the last round. By dinnertime I have unscrewed the bottom plate, added a drop of lead for extra weight, swung the club a dozen times, filed away half the fresh solder, found myself satisfied at last with the 3-

What other people find in poetry or art museums

wood, and begun to wonder what kind of fraction of an inch altera-
tion would make my putter more accurate.

If you are a golfer, you know what I mean. If you are about to
become a golfer, you will soon find out.

Many people—amateurs distressed by their failure to break 100, professionals weary of the travel and the strain of having to break par every day—swear to give up golf. Nobody ever does.

No other golf book, I believe, has ever started with the statement that golf is a simple game—or even that it is "deceptively simple," the phrase which I have used. But here, I think, is where those of us who have been writing about golf or teaching it have made a great mistake. We have been lured into too many complexities. We have forgotten that the game began with the very elemental discovery, by a Scotch shepherd who never had a lesson in his life, that he could knock a pebble an astounding distance with a good swift lick of his shepherd's crook—and that essentially the idea of the game even to-day is simply to pick up a stick and hit a ball with it, as straight and as hard as you can.

The trouble, I suppose, is that most people unfortunately do not take as naturally to swinging a golf stick as they do to throwing or hitting a baseball or knocking a tennis ball across a net. They usually have their difficulties at the beginning, and this makes them a gullible audience for anyone who has learned to play golf better. The game, therefore, lends itself to double-talk. We pros seem to be in the possession of all sorts of occult secrets denied to mere common men— so who can blame us if we stroke our beards and start discoursing pompously about the inside-out swing, turning in a barrel, starting the backswing with the shoulders, starting the downswing with the hips, pronating the wrists and all that sort of polysyllabic theory? I have seen golf books—you must have, too, if you have been interested in the game for any length of time—which were as difficult to read as advanced textbooks in physics, which in fact they somewhat resembled.

The temptation to talk and write like an oracle has been almost irresistible, and those who have succumbed to it (including me) were only being human. However, we have done golf a great disservice. We have made the game sound so difficult and so contrary to the body's natural instincts that surely we have scared away thousands of people who otherwise might have tried the game and enjoyed it. We have infected thousands of other people with inferiority complexes which have inhibited them from ever playing their best—and which, worst of all, have made them look upon a round of golf as an ordeal instead of a delight.

It is time now—and this is my reason for writing this book—to get back to first principles. Golf is a game, a great and glorious game, the greatest game any man was ever privileged to play. It is played for pleasure—for the modest and natural pleasure of walking around in the good clean air and for that other exquisite and almost unbearable pleasure of watching a perfect drive describe its graceful arc against a pure spring sky. Even those of us who earn our livings at the game, I can assure you, play it more for the pleasure than for the money.

Contrary to what many amateurs have been led to believe, the golf ball is not a natural enemy of mankind. It is by no means an evil spirit put there to confound you if you should happen to forget the merest detail of a long ritual of turning in a barrel, shifting the weight, pronating the wrists and writing the formula $E = mc^2$ on your mental blackboard. On the contrary, it is a friendly masterpiece of benign engineering skill, tightly wound, beautifully covered, gifted with great velocity, dimpled to make it fly straight and true; and its destiny is to sail away from earth in that perfect skybound parabola. It will gladly take wings if you give it half a chance. The next time you go out on a golf course, forget the fancy theory, shake your inferiority complex, give the ball a good healthy whack—and enjoy yourself. The game is a lot easier to play, and is a lot more fun, than the graybeards of the business have tried to pretend.

I learned this from my father, whom I consider one of the greatest teaching pros in the business. (And a pretty fair player, too, even today in his sixties.) My father has never liked to pretend that golf is as complicated as the blueprints for a spacecraft. Instead he has always preached this simple motto: "With a good grip, a little ability and a lot of desire, *anybody* can become a good golfer."

I probably first heard this common-sense remark at the age of four, when I began swinging a sawed-off club. It has been the entire foundation of my career and to this day it remains the most useful thing anybody has ever told me about golf. It can be the magic phrase, the open sesame, that will clear away the barriers that lie in anybody else's way to a good game of golf. Young or old, man or woman, scratch player, hacker or beginner who has never yet held a golf club, you can improve your present game or begin playing well from the start if you will paste these reassuring words in your golf cap.

The *grip*—as my father had the vision to see many years ago—is the most fundamental, most neglected single aspect of golf. Without the right grip on the club you can practice for years, you can develop a swing that is a perfect picture of grace and balance, yet never play within many strokes of your potential best—and you will have days when you can hardly play at all. With the right grip you can make all kinds of other mistakes, yet get away with them: a good grip is the cardinal virtue that can compensate for dozens of golfing sins. The strange thing is that, in my observation, only about one player in fifty uses the proper grip. Even some of the touring pros have never learned the simple secret of the grip; they hold onto the club in a manner that must cost them thousands of dollars of tournament money a year.

Ability, at least to the average player, is of minor importance. If you have played golf at all, you must have run into elderly men who can no longer hit the ball more than 150 yards or so at a crack, yet who consistently beat younger men in the prime of life and at the peak of their strength. You have seen one hundred pound women —like Marlene Bauer Hagge, Sandra Haynie and Barbara Romack— who can consistently beat all but a handful of the finest male players in the nation. True, among the very top professionals, physical size, strength and natural-born coordination make a difference. Gary Player might be unbeatable if he were two inches taller and weighed fifteen more pounds. Jerry Barber, who has the surest touch of anybody on and around the putting greens, might be unbeatable if he had been born with wrists a little larger around. But almost anybody can learn to play in the first flight at his country club or against the best players who patronize his public course. Any man without a serious physical handicap can learn to shoot in the 70s. Any woman can learn to shoot in the low 80s. There are blind golfers who play a good game, and legless golfers too.

A lot of desire, as my father says, is the key. Psychology, the mental approach, is a much greater factor in golf than has ever been fully appreciated. It wins and loses tournaments on the pro circuit, and it plays a far larger role than physical differences in determining which amateurs will shoot in the 70s and which will keep struggling vainly to break 100. Most golf books are long on photographs of how the weight should be distributed at the top of the swing and are short on the philosophy and strategy of golf. This book, as you already know if you have thumbed through its pages before starting to read, is short on rules about weight balance—which I have found lead to more confusion than improvement—and is long on the mental approach. For it is my earnest belief that a player must feel that he wants to play a very good game, else he will never play even a respectable game.

To quote my father once more, "Ninety per cent of golf is played from the shoulders up." The fundamentals of the grip and the swing are reasonably simple, even though widely misunderstood. The psychology of golf—demanding as it does its peculiar compromise between concentration and relaxation, between a fierce determination to conquer and a refusal to take any game too seriously—is far more complex. We can put it this way:

What you need to know in order to go out on a golf course for the first time—or to go out next time and beat your best previous score by many strokes—is as simple as the rules of checkers, which any child can learn in one session. But over and above these fundamentals, there is an art to golf which you need to know to enjoy it to the fullest and to realize your own full potential, and this art has as many combinations, permutations and variations on a theme as does chess. You will never master it—and neither, I fear, will any pro. The fun of the game, the fun which I constantly enjoy and which you too can learn to savor, is in trying.

The harder you work at playing the game—this sounds like a contradiction, but as we go along you will see what I mean—the more relaxed you will feel about it and the more you will love it. Moreover, the better you will play—better than you ever dreamed possible. There is a great deal to be said for the power of positive thinking in golf. The man who contents himself with hoping to break 100 probably never will. If the same man starts thinking about breaking 70, he actually has a chance.

Does it seem ridiculous to you—who have never before played a round of golf, or have played hundreds of rounds without breaking 80 or 90 or even 100—that you might some day shoot a round in the 60s? Bear with me, for the odds are not nearly as high as you think.

CHAPTER II

HOW TO BE
THE ONE GOLFER
IN FIFTY WHO HOLDS
THE CLUB RIGHT

TO THE BEGINNER, golf certainly can *seem* like a terribly difficult game. I have been through it myself and I know. (The discouraged beginner should remind himself from time to time that Palmer, Player, Nicklaus, Snead and every other pro who now competes in the tournaments were all beginners at one time, scarcely able to shoot par even if started 10 yards off the green.) The beginning golfer's first swing may barely nick the ball enough to make it trickle a slow 5 feet. In fact, the first swing often misses the ball entirely. The player who tries to learn by hitting balls at a driving range, as so many players do nowadays, may go there time after time, haul off at bucket after bucket of balls, and never once see that perfect parabola he is aiming for.

But this does not mean what many beginners have been led to believe, namely, that golf is such an artificial game that you must reverse the normal functioning of your body. The real reason golf is so difficult at the start is simply this:

The first thing a person does when he decides to give golf a try is to pick up a club. Unfortunately the "natural" way to pick it up—after years of holding baseball bats, suitcase handles, brooms or frying

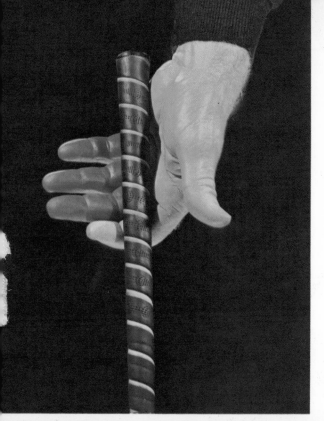

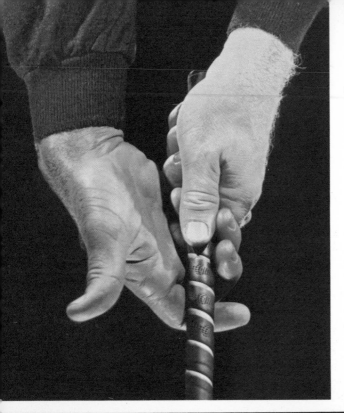

[LEFT] *The right palm can now fit firmly over the left thumb, with two fingers (red) applying pressure.*

[BELOW] *This view of my complete grip, and its mirrored images on both sides, shows the final position of the two hands.*

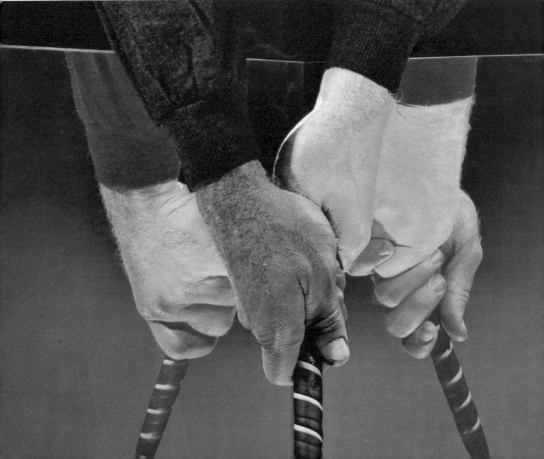

pans—is the wrong way. So the would-be player's career is ruined right then and there.

The grip is the crucial junction point from which all the body's strength and rhythm are transmitted to the club; it is like the gearbox where the horsepower in an automobile engine is coverted into revolutions of the wheels. When the beginning player picks up the club and sets the golfing habits of a lifetime, he jams the gear wheels together all cockeyed—and they are bound to clash, waste power and sometimes throw him into reverse for all the years to come. Unless, of course, he straightens them out, which is something that few players ever manage to do.

There is only one right way to grip a golf club. One must keep both hands locked together and working together, holding the club firmly enough to avoid even the slightest turning in the hands while at the same time leaving the muscles sufficiently relaxed for a nice easy swing—and there is only one possible way to accomplish this double objective.

It's not too easy to describe in words. While you're reading this, study the color pictures in this chapter, which show the right way to hold the club—and also the drawings.

As far as the left hand is concerned, it's the last three fingers that do the work. They have to hold the shaft tight against the palm—firmly enough so that it can't turn, yet not so tight as to get cramped and stiff. You lay the shaft diagonally across the left palm, from base of the index finger to the opposite corner, then close the last three fingers snugly. The forefinger and thumb play a secondary role. They help steady your hold on the club and give you the feel of it.

As far as the right hand is concerned, it's the two middle fingers that do the job. Like the last three fingers of the left hand, they apply the pressure—firm enough to keep the club from turning, but not unnaturally tight. The little finger of the right hand overlaps the index finger of the left hand and forms a link between the two, keeping them working together. (I'm talking, of course, about the Vardon overlapping grip which is used by virtually all of today's golfers; I'll have a word later about the slight variations found in the other two brands of grip.) The thumb and forefinger, like the thumb and forefinger of the left hand, help steady your grip and give you the feel of the club. But it's the middle two fingers that do most

RIGHT HAND   LEFT HAND

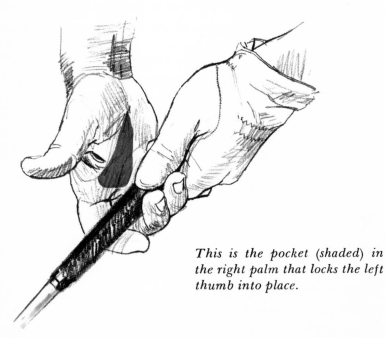

This is the pocket (shaded) in the right palm that locks the left thumb into place.

of the work—as you could see by looking at my right hand. I have heavy calluses running almost the entire length of the two middle fingers, and no calluses anywhere else on that hand.

There's one other thing to watch about the right hand. Notice, if you will, that if you start to close the fingers of your hand, as if about to make a fist, a little pocket forms in the palm; it runs from the heel of the hand—the lower left corner as you look at it—diagonally up toward the base of the index finger. This pocket is very important. When you put your right hand on the club, this pocket must fit over your left thumb. Then the part of your right hand lying below the thumb must close firmly, pressing against the left thumb with a good, snug hold.

If you're holding the club with the last three fingers of your left hand and the middle two fingers of your right hand, and if your left thumb is cradled firmly in that little pocket of your right hand, with the part of the right hand below the thumb keeping a steady pressure, then you've got it.

What you've done—you can see this for yourself—is firm up and consolidate your grip to the point where there is an absolute minimum of air space anywhere between your hand and the club. Your grip is so steady that the stress of the backswing isn't going to jar it loose at any point. Nor is the shock of impact when you hit the ball—a shock which is much more violent than most golfers realize. At the same time, you've got your hands nicely locked together so that they can work as a team. As your wrists start breaking on the backswing, they can move in perfect unison; they won't fight each other as they do in most bad grips. On the downswing, they are free to put all the whip of which your muscles are capable into the club.

I won't promise you that you'll be happy with your grip at the start. You can tell by looking at it that it's absolutely right, by all principles of physiology and engineering, but it probably won't feel good the first time you try it. (There's an old saying around golf courses that if a grip feels comfortable at the start, there's probably something wrong with it.) You may find that the two pressure fingers of your right hand aren't used to doing that kind of work and tend to get tired and sore; they may continue to be tender, in fact, until you've had time to build up some calluses. You may have trouble keeping the pressure on with your right hand below the thumb.

But, believe me, this is the right way to hold the club—and the only right way. Master it, and you're more than halfway home as a golfer. You'll have an asset which, as I have said, not more than one golfer in fifty possesses. And you will be able to commit a half-dozen other mistakes in your swing and still make the ball move.

Now about those other types of grip. There are two of them. One is the interlocking grip, in which the little finger of the right hand, instead of merely overlapping the left index finger, is stuck as far as it will go between the left index finger and the left second finger. (At the same time, of course, the left index finger goes between the little finger and the next finger of the right hand.) Some people have

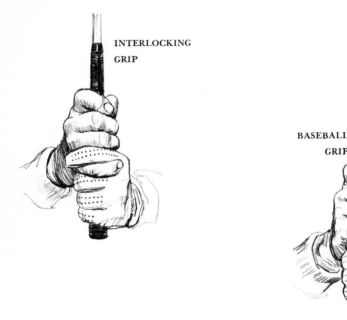

These two less common grips have some advantages for certain types of players.

found that it works for them—Lloyd Mangrum and Jack Nicklaus, for example, among the pros.

The other is the baseball grip. The hands don't overlap at all; they're put on the shaft of the club independently, although right next to one another. For some players I think that either the baseball or the interlocking grip has an advantage. If your hands are unusually weak or unusually small, often one or the other of these grips will help you get a better hold on the club. Many women, I think, would profit especially from using the baseball grip. So probably would many older players who have begun to get a touch of arthritis or rheumatism in their hands.

Both the interlocking and the baseball grips, however, are simply variations on a theme. You still have to apply pressure as you do with the Vardon grip. You make the last three fingers of the left hand and the middle two fingers of the right hand do the work, and you keep the below-thumb part of the right hand snug and firm. You eliminate the air spaces and keep the hands working together.

Now, then, about the Vs. I have left them until last because their importance has been stressed so much in recent golf teaching that the basic principle of the grip has been neglected. They're important, all right—but they're a refinement of the grip, not the fundamental part of it.

The Vs are the angles formed by your thumbs and forefingers as you grip the club, and where they point depends on where you've placed your hands on the shaft. The standard advice given by most pros and in most golf books is that you should place the left hand on the shaft so that when you look down on it, from the position in which you address the shot, you can see two knuckles—the knuckle of the index finger and the one next to it. Then, after you have put your right hand on the club, you should see plainly that the Vs of both hands are pointing toward your right shoulder.

This is a useful generalization, as true as most generalizations—but it can get you in trouble.

A little golfing theory is in order here. As you take your swing at the ball, your arms, wrists and hands are going to move in whatever way is natural to them. When you get down to the hitting area and make contact with the ball, the hands will always tend to be in the same position, time after time.

Now then:

If you address the ball with your hands somewhat toward the right as they lie on the club—that is to say, with those Vs aimed at the point of your right shoulder, or even beyond—then your hands, as they move into their natural position in the hitting area, will be opening the face of the club a little.

21

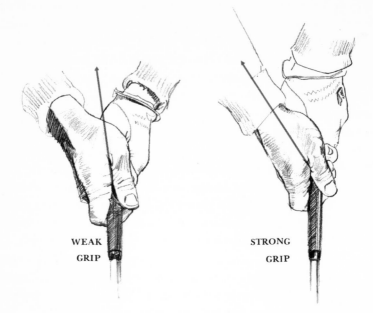

WEAK GRIP

STRONG GRIP

Moving the Vs controls hook or slice. The strong grip
is better for amateurs.

When the Vs point well to the right, we call it a "strong" grip. By closing the clubface at the point of impact, the strong grip tends to overcome any natural tendency to slice.

When the Vs point straight up and down, we call it a "weak" grip. By opening the clubface at the point of impact, this weak grip tends to overcome any natural tendency to hook.

So the fact of the matter is that no two golfers should ever see exactly the same number of knuckles on the left hand. The ideal number for you may just happen to be two, as the guidebook says— but it is much more likely to be some queer fraction like 2.367 or 1.835. Your Vs should perhaps point to the seam of your sweater on your right shoulder or to the open air a little beyond that—or perhaps they should point to your Adam's apple. Every player is a little different, and even the same player may change from time to time.

Most professional golfers have a natural tendency to hook the ball. (A tendency to hook is a great asset. All other things being equal, the beginner who finds that he hooks the ball right from the start will turn out to be a better golfer than the beginner who slices it.) Playing day in and day out, moreover, develops the hands and wrists, and this further encourages a hook. So a great many pros use the weak grip. You can see in all the photographs in this book that my own grip is very much in this direction. The V of my left hand usually points to my chin, the V of my right hand to the inside of my right shoulder.

Most weekend amateurs have a tendency to slice and should use the strong grip. This would be particularly true at the start of the season, after a long winter in which the golfing muscles were never used. It would be less true in the middle of a long vacation during which the amateur was playing every day. At such a time, when lots of golf has toned up his muscles, he will almost surely start hooking the ball unless he moves his hands a little to the left. The best way to find out for sure where the Vs should point is to take some lessons and get your pro's advice. The only other way is through trial and error. If you are consistently slicing, move the Vs to the right. If you are consistently hooking, move them to the left.

But don't let those phrases strong grip and weak grip mislead you. They have nothing to do with the amount of pressure you apply with your hands. Whether you use the strong or the weak, you still have to keep a steady hold on the club—not so tight that you feel as if you're squeezing it to death, not so tight that your muscles get locked, but tight enough so that even if you hit a hidden stone the club wouldn't turn in your hands.

Some people find they can hold onto the club better if it has a leather grip; others prefer rubber. A few golfers like to hold the club in their bare hands, but most find they can grip it better with a glove on the left hand—either a half glove that leaves the top two joints of the fingers uncovered or a full glove that covers everything. Many golfers like to keep the handles of their clubs tacky, with one of the wax or resin preparations you can buy in any pro shop or sporting goods store. Other golfers find that this is only an annoyance.

I myself use leather grips and keep them tacky. I wear a full glove on my left hand for all shots until I get to the green, then take it off because I think I get a better feel of the putter barehanded. But these are all matters of individual preference. My advice would be to try all of them—and anything new that may come along—then go with what seems to suit you best. As in so much of golf, your guide should be the way you feel. If some wax on the handle makes you feel that you're holding the club better, by all means use it—and keep using it. If it only distracts you and makes you feel uncomfortable, forget it.

CHAPTER III

THE HEAD AND FEET:
YOUR ANCHOR POINTS

AFTER THE GRIP comes the second fundamental: the matter of what you do with your head and feet. We have to talk about them before we can talk about the swing because they are the anchor points around which the entire swing revolves. Unless you've got your feet firmly planted on the turf and your head firmly fixed at one definite spot in space, your swing can't be any good. Talking about the swing before talking about the head and feet would be like trying to build a house without a foundation.

Let's talk first about the feet because they're easier to control. I don't think there's much you have to worry about as far as your feet are concerned, just a few very simple and elemental matters. I don't go along with the golf teachers who talk at great length about the finer points of the stance and give detailed instructions about holding the left foot at a 30-degree angle from the line of flight, all that sort of thing.

About all you really have to worry about is feeling comfortable. You don't want your feet so far apart that they'll keep you from turning your body smoothly. Nor do you want them too close together, for this also would tie you up and restrict your swing. If you just sort of stand up to the ball naturally, you'll find that your stance tends to be about as wide as your shoulders when you're using a driver. Then, as you move down to the shorter clubs, your feet tend of their own accord to move closer together, until they're perhaps no more than 6 inches apart when you're choking the pitching wedge for a little 30-yarder.

As far as the angle of your feet is concerned, they'll be all right if you just get set in the position that seems to be the best balanced, the least awkward. Ordinarily, the way most golfers do it, the left foot is at a slight angle, with the toe pointed out. The right foot is either more or less perpendicular to the line of flight or also pointed a little. It doesn't matter too much, ordinarily, if the feet are pointed a little more or a little less. Unless a pro tells you that for some perverse reason you have a tendency to hold your feet in a position that ties you up, or have somehow fallen into the habit of doing it—or unless you yourself have noticed that you feel terribly uncomfortable over the ball—you can forget it.

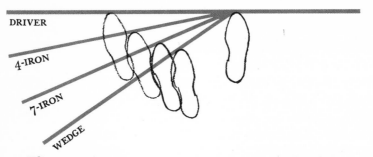

The stance gets narrower and more open as the clubs range from driver to wedge.

You know about the open stance and the closed stance, of course. Ordinarily, the stance with the wedge is quite open; the left foot is moved well back from the intended line of flight. Then, as you go to the longer clubs, the stance gradually closes, a little more with each club. With the driver, the stance is completely square, with the feet planted evenly on the line of flight, or somewhat closed, with the right foot drawn back from the line. Again, this seems to be something that usually happens by itself. Most golfers just naturally feel more comfortable over a wedge shot when the stance is open, and more comfortable on the tee when the stance is square or closed. You might take notice of the position of your feet sometime, when you're hitting shots off the practice tee, and see if they're working this way. In all probability, they are and you can forget them. If not, then try opening and closing your stance and see if you can get more comfortable.

A big part of feeling good over the ball is to have the feet planted solidly from toe to heel, like a brick sitting in the turf. You don't want your weight balance too much on the ball of the foot or too much on the heel; you want it distributed evenly; you want all those spikes dug in, nice and firmly. To achieve this, you've got to flex your knees a little; you've got to be "sitting down to the ball," as the saying goes. Actually you're standing just about as you might if you were making the first move to sit down in a chair. Or as if you were water skiing. Your knees are flexed just enough to make your legs feel flexible and relaxed. They're all set to help you make a smooth easy turn as you start your swing.

As you stand up to the ball, you're not so far away that you have to crouch to reach it nor so close that you have to stand stiffly upright. You're bent forward just a little at the waist and your arms seem to

In the correct stance, the golfer bends slightly, but he does not reach for the ball.

The correct stance, seen from the right side, reveals flexed knees and good balance.

hang naturally and comfortably from your shoulders. Again it seems to me that the right way to do it is the natural way and the easy way, but you may want to check yourself against the drawing, because this is the part of the stance which seems to cause more trouble than any other for the average golfer. Many amateurs seem to want to make the golf swing harder than it is; they stand too far from the ball, which makes them crouch and bend too far. (Or maybe it's that they crouch too far, which makes them stand too far from the ball.) At any rate, you see far more people standing bent too far over the ball than standing too erect. This throws their weight forward onto the balls of their feet and gets them completely off-balance. You can't swing well unless your feet are planted so firmly from heel to toe, and your weight is so evenly in balance that you feel like a basketball player standing on guard and ready to move in either direction, right or left.

This is the one aspect of the stance that seems prone to give the most trouble, and you'll have to watch it. Aside from that, there's not much to worry about as far as the feet are concerned.

If only this were true of the head! But the head is a different matter entirely. You can't consistently execute a good golf shot unless you keep your head entirely still over the ball—and holding the head still isn't easy. Even the pros gifted with a maximum of natural ability have had to spend years concentrating on holding the head steady; nevertheless they continue to move it from time to time and have to keep reminding themselves all over again. Some golfers never do learn to hold their heads steady, and thus spend a lifetime of frustration at the game.

Let me tell you why the head is so important.

The head and feet are your anchor points. You can think of your body as a pole running between these two points, and your arms and the club as a string which holds a stone—the clubhead—that revolves around the pole. As long as the pole stays steady, the stone will follow the same path, time after time. You aim it at the ball and it hits the ball, dead center. But if the pole tilts, goodbye. The path of the stone is thrown off. It never hits the ball dead center. It hits too high or too low, or to the left or the right. It can even miss the ball entirely. Every time you see a beginning golfer whiff, you know for sure that he has moved his head. It's got to be the head. A golfer can't move his feet, at least not without superhuman effort. So the only way you can possibly tilt that pole is to move the head.

If you lift your head during the swing, you're bound to top the ball; it's lifting the head that accounts for all those deep cuts or "smiles" that beginning golfers keep putting through the covers of the ball. At best, if you don't actually top the ball with the bottom edge of the club, you'll get nothing more than a very low, flat shot, with no distance.

If you lower your head during the swing, you've got to hit behind the ball—or, at best, hit it "fat," taking a lot of turf at the moment of impact and ballooning it up like a little pop fly.

If you move your head to the left, you get a drastic hook.

If you move your head to the right, you can also get a hook—or, more likely, a bad slice or push to the right.

I can't emphasize too strongly how important the head is. I can only tell you that when you see a really bad shot on the golf course—a screaming hook or roundhouse slice that goes out of bounds, or a ball that is topped and dribbles a mere 10 yards, or a little pop fly that goes only a tenth of the intended distance—it means ninety-nine times out of a hundred that the golfer moved his head. The majority of amateurs move their heads on most of their shots, and even we pros have to guard all the time against head motion.

Many golfers think it's easy to keep the head steady; they think that all you have to do is keep your eye on the ball. Thus, when the amateur tops a shot, his friends like to say, "You looked up." When he hits behind, they say, "You didn't have your eye on it."

They're wrong. At least they're mostly wrong. The only thing they're right about is that some golfers do have a tendency to peek; these players will top shots, especially shots up close to the green, because they lift their heads to look up and see where the ball has gone before they've hit it. But, although you can move your head as a result of taking your eye off the ball, the reverse of this, unfortunately, is not true. Keeping your eye on the ball is absolutely no guarantee at all that you will hold your head steady. Your eyes and head work entirely independently. You can hold stock still in the chair where you are now reading this book and roll your eyes around in their sockets to look at the floor, left wall, ceiling or right wall. You can focus your eyes on a doorknob, get up out of your chair and, without once taking your eyes off the knob, walk all around the room, lie on the floor or stand on a chair. If that isn't moving your head while "keeping your eye on the ball," what is?

So it isn't enough just to keep your eye on the ball. You must consciously and deliberately force your head to hold still. And it isn't easy at all. It takes prolonged effort and concentration. It is probably the hardest part of golf to learn.

Like everybody else who plays golf, I was once a confirmed head mover. I swayed to the left and I swayed to the right. (The temptation to sway to the left, I have discovered, is strongest when you're trying to overpower the ball, to hit it farther than usual. The temptation to sway to the right is strongest when you are trying to get it up in the air fast, as when there are trees in front of you.) I lowered my head and hit the ball too far, or raised my head and half topped it, with catastrophic results.

I don't do it any more—at least not very often. In fact I suppose that holding my head still is the best thing I do at golf. I've been happy to note, in series after series of pictures of my swing (such as the one facing page 33), that my head stays just as steady as if I had it in a vise. I don't move it a fraction of an inch on the backswing nor a fraction of an inch on the downswing, not until long after the ball is in the air. So I don't miss too many shots. I can concentrate now on the finer points of the swing.

If everybody could learn to hold his head still, there wouldn't be any golfers around still trying vainly to break 100. In fact, there wouldn't be any 90 shooters. Everybody would be playing in the 70s or the low 80s. This would be a really happy country.

I wish I could give you Ten Easy Rules for how to do it, but I can't. I fought the problem for years. I worked on my grip until I had it perfected and could forget it. I learned to get comfortable over the ball, so that I could forget my feet. I learned about the compact swing—that's relatively easy, as you'll see in the next chapter—and quit worrying about that part of the game. Then I concentrated on holding my head still. I thought about it almost every time I hit the ball, in practice or out on the golf course, for month after month. I made up my mind to hold steady. When I moved on a shot, I forced myself to do better the next time.

Getting comfortable over the ball is part of it: if you've got a nice balance and your feet are good and firm, you have a far better chance to hold steady. Relaxation is part of it: if your body movements flow free and easy, there's no irresistible physical force to pull you off your axis and make you sway. But it's mostly a matter of concentration: you've got to be determined to hold steady. After that it's a matter of practice.

Some people say you should swing a club in front of a mirror and watch to see that your head stays steady. Some people say you should turn your back to the sun and swing your club while watching your shadow. I don't agree. While you're swinging at the golf ball, you've got to have your eye on the ball. The swing you take while watching a mirror or your shadow isn't the same.

Some people say you can learn to keep your head from lifting by practicing with one end of a handkerchief tied in your belt and the other end held in your teeth. I don't believe this at all.

I don't think there is any mechanical method or short cut in the world which will help you keep your head steady. You've just got to think about it and practice it until it becomes second nature. Or almost second nature. You can never forget the head entirely. If I didn't keep reminding myself to keep my head steady, I'd go right back to moving it.

You don't have to look in a mirror or watch your shadow to know if you are moving your head. You can get a better reading by taking a lesson and asking your pro. You can even judge by results. I'd say as a rule of thumb that if you've got a halfway decent grip and are still shooting over 90, you're almost surely moving your head, and have been doing it ever since you took up the game. If you used to shoot in the 70s but have gone up into the 80s, you've surely reacquired the habit. If you're consistently hooking the ball badly or slicing it or topping it or hitting behind it, there can't be any doubt.

You'll have to work at it. All I can do is wish you good concentration—and good luck. For if you've acquired a sound grip and then can just manage to keep your head steady, the rest of the mechanical side of golf is a breeze.

In the photograph on the facing page, I am taking the club straight back "in one piece." (See page 34)

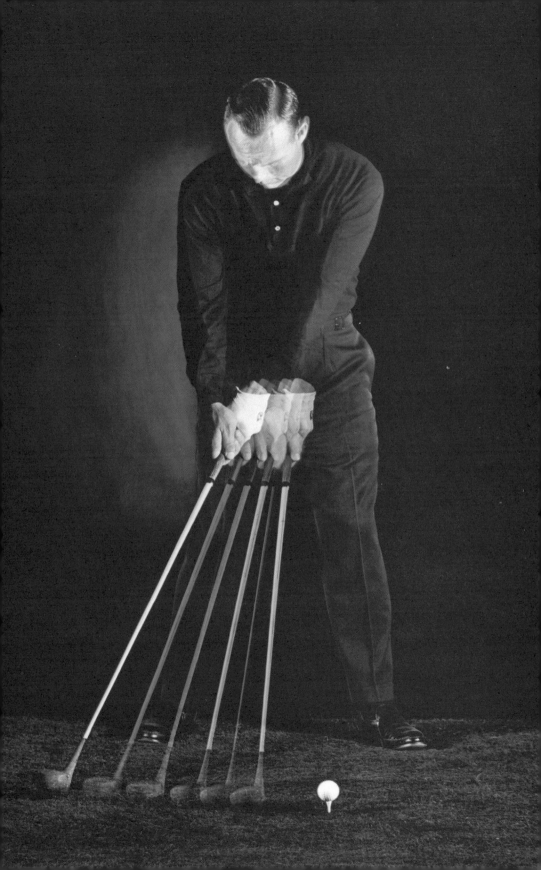

The big "turn" is right for me, but I never think about it.
I do think about keeping my head still.

CHAPTER IV

HOW TO SWING HARDER
WHILE TRYING LESS

As YOU MAY HAVE OBSERVED if you have ever watched me play, I have one of the biggest "turns" in golf. By this I mean that when I take the clubhead back, my whole body rotates far to the right, until I have practically turned my back to the spot where I am aiming the ball. My left hip swings way around; so do my shoulders.

Did I plan my swing that way? No, I never did. Neither did my father when he was teaching me the game. In fact, at one of my early professional tournaments when many of the other pros were seeing me play for the first time, one of them nudged my father, who was also watching me, and asked, "Did you teach him that turn?" My father replied, "Now wouldn't that have been a silly thing to do?"

What he meant was that a teaching pro should never urge his pupils to think one way or another about the turn, and the golfer himself should never worry about whether he is making a large turn or a small one. I certainly never worry about it. One reason I know I have a big turn is that other golfers have told me; also I have seen it for myself in pictures. I have this kind of turn because it comes natural to me. Given my kind of physique and the kind of physical condition that comes from playing nearly every day, my hands and arms just naturally pull my body around into a big turn when I take the clubhead back.

A big turn is a wonderful asset in golf for the turn generates your power, and the bigger the turn the greater the power. But it's not something you should plan or worry about. If your leg, torso and shoulder muscles have the strength and agility to give you a big turn, you'll have a big turn. If not, you'll have to settle for a little less.

As a matter of fact, almost everything that has been written or discussed about the golf swing—all the millions of words devoted to the turn, the pivot and the weight shift—have been unnecessarily complicated and confusing. I urge you to forget them and start your thinking all over, for the truth about the swing is just this:

The swing is the easiest part of golf. Once you've got the right grip—and if you hold your head steady—it is almost physically impossible to swing badly. There are two rules and two rules only that you have to remember, and they are so simple and natural that you can make them part of your second nature in a mere half hour on the practice tee.

Rule No. 1 is to take the club back, as you start your backswing, *smoothly and without breaking your wrists*. You have to take it straight back "in one piece," as they say around the golf course, without any wrist action at all. Do this for the first 12 inches that the clubhead moves—as in the photograph facing page 32—and you've got the swing practically licked.

Starting the club this way gets your entire body into the act. To take the club back in one piece you have to use your leg muscles, your torso muscles, your shoulders. Your body gets started on a nice, easy, well-coordinated pattern of motion, from feet to shoulders. And now you can forget everything else you've ever heard about how the body and arms are supposed to behave during the swing—for once you are past that crucial first 12 inches, you would have to be a "genius" to manage to do anything wrong.

Do you have to worry about shifting your weight? Of course not. All the standard advice about shifting the weight to the right foot when starting the backswing, and shifting back to the left foot on the downswing, is completely unnecessary. It's worse than that; it's confusing and harmful. Whoever it was that first thought of giving this advice to beginners has caused more aggravation and agony than the common cold.

If your grip is correct, if you hold your head steady and if you take the club back in one piece, your weight just naturally shifts to the right foot. You can't help shifting your weight. You don't have to think about it any more than you have to think which foot to move next when you're walking.

The same thing happens in reverse when you have swung the clubhead back as far as you can and get ready to hit the ball. As you start your downswing, your weight just naturally shifts to your left foot. You can't help it. If you didn't shift your weight, you'd be standing there with your arms in the air the rest of the day.

What must have happened, somewhere back in golfing history, is that some theoretician noticed that golfers shift their weight in this manner and promptly decided to turn it into a law. But in putting the facts into a rule of instruction, he got them backward. Instead of saying what was the simple truth, namely, that when you take your backswing your weight shifts to the right foot and when you take your downswing your weight shifts to the left foot, he made everybody nervous by claiming that you've got to shift your weight to swing properly. What had always been a perfectly easy and natural body movement suddenly became a self-conscious, awkward chore. It was as if he had announced, "To breathe properly, one must always exhale after inhaling, and must always inhale after exhaling." You breathe in and out from the moment of birth without ever thinking about it—in fact, you do it in your sleep—but once you start worrying about it, it gets to be a problem.

What is true about the weight shift is also true about the turn or pivot. The theoreticians are correct when they say that the golf swing is like "turning in a barrel" or "turning like a barber pole." If you think of yourself as having an imaginary pole running from your head to your feet, it's correct that this pole simply revolves on its axis, first to the right on your backswing, then to the left on the downswing. The pole doesn't sway or shift laterally. But you don't have to think about this to achieve it. You can't possibly take a backswing, if you keep your head steady and start the club back as I have described, without turning your body. Your hips just naturally pivot; your shoulders just naturally come around. About the only way you can manage to do it wrong is to start thinking about it—like the man on the tightrope who never falls unless he starts getting self-conscious about which foot to pick up next.

35

If you will just trust your instincts on the matter of the weight shift and the turn, you will be all right. As a matter of fact, you are stuck with your instincts anyway. The human physique is simply too complicated to be controlled by anything except its own marvelous system of nerves and reflexes. If you try controlling it with your brain, you are out of luck. You can't order your body, "Digest that food, stomach," "Beat slower, heart," "Secrete more gall, liver"—and neither can you successfully think yourself into the right position at the top of your backswing. If you start saying to yourself, "Hold that weight, right foot," "Pivot there, left hip," "Get around there, left shoulder"—if you do this, the whole complicated movement will fall to pieces.

Rule No. 2 is to *keep the club under control* at all times or, to use a phrase that I like, to keep the swing *compact*. It's an easy, natural rule to follow—at least it should be; yet, strangely, even many pros violate it at times, and most amateurs violate it most of the time.

We all like to hit the ball as far as we can, and the best way to hit it a mile seems to be to take the biggest possible windup. I say "seems." What the natural human urge for power often does is make us strain too hard, take too big a backswing, lose control of the club—and dissipate our power completely.

Each of us has his own limits. We can take the club back just so far and no farther. For most pros the distance is considerable; many of them have such a long backswing that the club goes up and around all the way to the horizontal and even past the horizontal, until it is actually dipping toward the earth. Only a few amateurs—the strongest of them, with muscles and joints kept loose through constant exercise—can hope to duplicate this kind of swing. Most amateurs cannot take the club back nearly so far as the horizontal. Many of them would play better golf if they never tried to take it past the perpendicular.

You've got to keep the swing compact and well within your physical capabilities. The minute you feel that you are stretching yourself on the backswing, the minute you feel that you are fighting the weight of the club instead of remaining easily in control of it, you have swung too far. And when you go too far, one of two things happens. Either you bend your left elbow or you loosen your grip. Either way you are lost.

36

CORRECT   INCORRECT

Bending the left elbow is one of the few errors that must be consciously avoided.

Bending the left elbow is the common error of beginners and also, I have noticed, of older golfers who are still trying to take the same kind of backswing that they took when their muscles and joints were more flexible. At least one out of every four amateurs, it has been my observation, bends the left elbow consistently or at least on every shot where he is trying for extra distance.

Loosening the grip is a fault so common that it even affects the pros. The arms go up, around and back as far as they can. Still the player is not satisfied; he feels he should wind up a little more; he strives to get the club down past that horizontal line. If he keeps his left arm straight—as all good golfers do through instinct and long training—there is only one way he can get the club to move any farther. He has to let loose with his hands and let the club wobble of its own weight. Some golfers let loose with the thick part of the right hand beneath the thumb. Others make an even more deadly mistake: they actually let go with the last three fingers of the left hand.

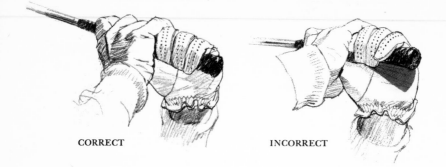

CORRECT   **INCORRECT**

Loosening the left-hand grip at the top of the back-swing (see shaded area on right) is a common and quite serious mistake.

Almost all the British pros I have seen in tournament play tend to loosen their grip at the top of the backswing. The reason, I suspect, is that they get to play less often than do our American pros. Their golfing season does not last nearly so long as ours, which goes virtually year round. Even at the height of their season, they do not get the opportunity of playing every day. Lacking the lubrication of joint and tendon that can only come from constant practice, they are physically unable to take the club back as far as American pros. Yet they know that it takes power to win any modern golf tournament. Striving for it, they let go of the club.

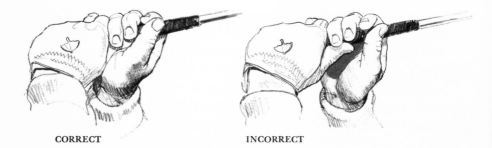

CORRECT   **INCORRECT**

If not held firmly in place, the right hand also will open up, destroying the smoothness of the swing.

38

How to Swing Harder While Trying Less

I once fell into the habit. In 1958, after the Professional Golfers Association tournament in Philadelphia, in which I finished a miserable distance behind Dow Finsterwald, I went home to Latrobe and played round after round with my father, just the two of us, trying to figure out what had gone wrong with my game. Neither he nor I could solve the mystery. I had some photographs made. As nearly as we could see, I was gripping the club the way I always had gripped it, and was swinging the same way. Then one day, while I was practicing some little pitch shots, the answer came to me. At the top of my backswing for pitch shots, I had a different feeling in my hands from the feeling on longer shots. The club felt better in my hands; I was more in control. There could be only one explanation: on the long shots I was letting go.

The way I was loosening my grip was nothing spectacular, nothing at all like the exaggerated letting go which is characteristic of beginning players. What I was doing did not even show up in the pictures I had had made. My father, who has an eagle eye for golfing defects, had not been able to detect it. I had never suspected it. But it was enough to throw off my game completely.

It does not take much loosening of the fingers to ruin a golf shot. Once you have relaxed your grip at the top of your backswing you have to tighten it again—and it would take a miracle to put your fingers back in the exact same spot where they were before. They may not *seem* to have moved, the difference may be only a thousandth of an inch—but even the breadth of a single hair is enough to do the damage. The shaft of the club has turned in your hands, be it ever so slightly, and the clubhead can never possibly strike the ball in that precise straight line for which you are aiming.

About nine golfers out of ten loosen their grip at the top of the backswing. It is the most common single error in golf, next to gripping the club improperly to begin with, and it is the saddest error of all because there is absolutely nothing that it could possibly accomplish. You can't get a bit of extra distance out of the extra few inches that you achieve by wobbling the fingers. All you can get is trouble.

This whole matter of length is a lot less important than everybody seems to think. Among the pros, to be sure, it does make a difference. But the pros have to struggle constantly to get every last ounce of power into their shots. They are engaged in a game of inches. They are not just shooting to come up with a respectable 75 or even just to equal par; instead they are fighting to win tournaments by being a mere quarter of a stroke better each eighteen holes than the nearest opponent. That's how close it is among the pros, so they have to try anything that will add even a few feet to their shots. To the amateur, however, even the best of amateurs, 5 yards more or less on a drive means very little. To the average player, it means nothing at all. The man who shoots around 100 isn't suffering primarily from lack of power; he's simply dubbing too many shots.

With the irons, distance means even less than with the woods, for the irons aren't distance clubs at all. They're accuracy clubs. You're not trying to see how far you can powder the ball; you're trying to see how close you can lay it to the pin. And to show you something very important about the irons, I arranged an experiment which is shown in the drawings opposite.

Please take a good look at them for they contain a moral which every golfer should remember. In all of them I am using a 5-iron. In the drawing on the far right, I am taking what for me is a slightly fuller than usual backswing with this club; the shaft, as you can see, has gone back nearly to horizontal. In the middle drawing, I am at the top of a three-quarter swing. At the far left, I am taking a half swing; the club has gone back merely to the perpendicular.

From each of these backswings—the quite full, the three-quarter and the half swing—I then took my normal cut at the ball. I don't mean to say that I hit the ball as hard as I could because I never do this with an iron; I always stay a little within myself, for greater accuracy, But I did hit the ball as hard as I normally would hit it. And here is the interesting and significant thing:

With my full swing, a half-dozen shots made during the experiment averaged 165 yards.

With the three-quarter swing, my average was 160 yards.

With the half swing, my average was 150 yards.

What the experiment proves is that the length of the backswing makes very little difference in distance. Enlarging the arc of my swing all the way from the perpendicular to the nearly horizontal—a really tremendous difference in length of backswing—merely added

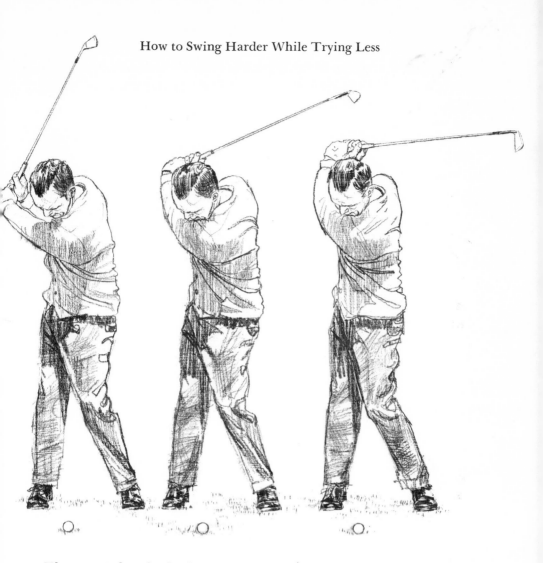

The arcs of these backswings are very different, but the half-swing shown at the far left will hit the ball almost as far as the full swing at the right.

15 yards to my shot. I could have accomplished the same thing by going to a 4-iron instead of a 5-iron.

The moral, of course, is that you don't have to press for that extra couple of inches in backswing—thereby running the risk of committing those two fatal errors of bending the left elbow or loosening the grip—to get enough distance to be a good golfer. You will get more distance, on the average, if you don't press.

41

Keep that swing *compact*. Don't let the club get away from you. The minute you feel you are stretching or straining on the back-swing, quit trying so hard.

This advice, I know, sounds contrary to everything that has been written and said about power golf in recent years; it even seems to oppose the way all the pros, including myself, play the game.

These contradictions, however, are only apparent, not real. All the pros, with a very few exceptions, use the compact swing: the kind of swing they take is well under control and well within physical limits —for *them*. (The few exceptions have such tremendous power and agility in their wrists that they can make up just before the moment of impact for any excesses of backswing.) My own swing, though it involves the big turn I spoke of and carries the club way back to below the horizontal at times, is a compact swing—*for me*. I never feel a sense of strain at the top of my backswing. I never let my left elbow bend. Not since that 1958 tournament in which I failed so badly have I loosened my grip on the club.

The pros play golf three hundred days a year. Some of them, I guess, play 365 days a year. They have the physical equipment and the physical condition to take a long, full way-around backswing.

The average amateur, playing forty or fifty times a year at most, will never have his golfing muscles in the same condition as the pros. He has to adjust the swing to his own capabilities. If he tries to exceed them, he will not add any distance—but will surely fall into those two common and cardinal errors of the bent elbow or the loosened fingers.

If you want to keep trying to lengthen your backswing—while still keeping your swing *compact*—good for you. I believe in playing the game to the hilt. And, as you play more frequently, as you become more relaxed and more confident, you will probably find your muscles and joints moving more smoothly and flexibly; you will then be able to lengthen the arc of your swing while still keeping firm control. Go to it, and more power to you!

On the other hand, if you are just an occasional golfer, playing a couple of times a month, you probably will find that you can score better using a half or three-quarter swing than if you take a full windup and run the risk of letting the club get away from you. Try it the next time you go out. Remind yourself before every shot to take something less than a full swing. On your iron shots, use a lower-numbered club if necessary. If you've been in the 90s or over, I'll make you a little bet that you shoot five to ten strokes better than your average.

Every country club has a few members who, in apparent defiance of all rules of logic, get better in the years after fifty when they are well past their peak of physical strength. Their secret lies in the facts we have been discussing. Realizing that their shoulders have tightened up and that they can no longer take the club back as far as they used to, they have deliberately settled for a three-quarter swing, or even a half swing.

This automatically makes them obey Rule 2 for the golf swing. Their swing is always compact; they never lose control; they never loosen their grip. At the same time, getting older has helped them follow Rule 1. Their wrists are no longer agile enough to pick up the club quickly; they just naturally have to take the clubhead back "in one piece," slowly and easily.

They have lost a little distance, which is not very important to the 80 or 90 shooter, and in return have gained immeasurably in accuracy, which is terribly important. An accurate player who never gets off the fairway and can hit the greens can easily shoot 85 even if he never knocks the ball more than 150 yards.

If you don't believe it, let me suggest another experiment. Sometime when you're feeling nice and relaxed on a good warm Saturday and aren't playing for blood, go out on the course with nothing longer than a 6-iron in your bag. Just take along your 6-, 7-, 8- and 9-irons, your wedge and your putter. Now you can't possibly hit the ball more than about 150 yards. You may think you're playing under a horrible handicap—but let's just see how many strokes it adds to your score.

Unless you are an exceptionally good golfer with a consistently long and accurate drive, I think you'll be surprised how few strokes it adds. You may even find yourself with your best score of the season.

What about the "upright" swing versus the "flat" swing? This is something I wish we didn't have to discuss at all, but you hear so much talk about it that I suppose we can't avoid it.

The upright swing, as you doubtless know, is one with an arc that tends to be almost perpendicular to the ground, with the club going almost straight up on the backswing, then almost straight down again. The flat swing is much more tilted—not as flat as the swing of a baseball bat which is virtually horizontal, but definitely tending in that direction.

Most of the books say that you should keep striving for an upright swing, that the flat swing is bad. Well, I just don't believe it. Jack Nicklaus gets good results with one of the most upright swings ever seen in professional golf, and Doug Ford has had great results over the years with a swing that is almost as flat as a pancake. My own swing is definitely on the flat side. But I never planned it that way; nor, I'm sure, did Nicklaus or Ford. This is just the natural way for us to swing.

I will say this; if you go too far to the extreme in either direction, if your swing is *too* upright or *too* flat, you may have trouble—especially as you get older. You see very few senior golfers with either an extremely upright or an extremely flat swing. If they started with one, they've changed—or they dropped out of the game because they couldn't change and found they could no longer play well as they got older.

But, in general, I don't think you should worry about it. Unless your pro tells you that you've gone to one extreme or the other and had better move back toward the happy medium, the only sensible thing to do about the argument over the upright versus the flat swing is to forget it. Almost always, a tendency in either direction is merely the natural result of physical build. Do what comes naturally and let the other fellows argue the theory. As long as they keep worrying about it, and also about shifting the weight and turning in a barrel, you will beat them every time.

The same goes for all the talk about where you should break your wrists on the backswing. I'm sure you've heard the discussions. Some people say you should never let them break until your hands have moved around past your right knee, others that you should wait until your hands are as high as your hips.

All I can say is that if you start the clubhead back without any wrist action and get past that crucial first 12 inches, you don't have to worry. If you asked me at what point in the backswing my own wrists begin to break, I'd have to tell you that I don't know. I don't want to know. I can't think of any single piece of knowledge that would help

44

me less, or be more likely to confuse me. My wrists start to break at the point where it becomes natural to them—and yours will do the same thing for you. Forget about them.

The whole thing about the golf swing is that it is a lot easier and a lot more natural than has been advertised. You don't have to worry about making a turn or pivot. If you will just follow Rule 1 and take the club back in one piece while keeping your head steady, your body will just naturally turn; you can't help turning. You don't have to worry about shifting your weight. As you start turning, your weight just naturally shifts to your right foot and, as you start the downswing, it just naturally shifts to the left foot. You don't have to strive for an upright swing as opposed to a flat swing. Unless you're the rare exception, the club is going to take the arc that is natural to you and best for your game. You don't have to worry about deliberately breaking your wrists. They'll break without any help from you.

I forgot one thing, didn't I? That's the matter of the inside-out swing, another of the ideals we are always urged to strive for. Well, as long as you start the club back in one piece, I'd like to see you swing any way *but* inside out. You can't help it. You don't have to worry about it any more than you have to worry about breathing out and breathing in.

Start the club back in one piece, without any wrist action for the first 12 inches. And, as you continue back, keep in control of the club; keep your swing compact. Don't try to strain back so far that you bend that elbow or loosen your grip. Everything else will take care of itself. There is only one real secret to the successful golf swing, aside from Rule 1 and Rule 2, and that is to be natural and relaxed.

It comes from practice which must necessarily, in the logical order of things, be our next topic.

CHAPTER V

HOW TO PRACTICE FOR
FUN AND PROFIT

I BEGIN THIS CHAPTER with misgivings—for I am well aware, from my own experience and from what teaching pros have told me, how difficult it is to persuade the average player to practice. This is hard for me to understand, but I know it's true. Perhaps it's because a round of golf with three enjoyable companions is a social event as well as a sport, whereas practice is generally a lone-wolf sort of thing.

So I'm not going to start out by telling you how much practice will improve your game, because you've doubtless heard this before and have been unimpressed. Instead I'm going to try to convince you that practice can be one of the most enjoyable parts of golf.

Let me tell you that I've known golfers who played for ten or fifteen years without ever practicing, never even considered practicing, thought it was a bore and a waste of time and then, for some reason, possibly because they had a free afternoon and couldn't find a match, finally happened to spend some time on the practice tee. They discovered how much fun it was and now they spend more time practicing than they do on the course.

Let me try to tell you my own feelings about practice. I love it. You can stand at the practice tee—try it some time—and, in your mind's eye, play an entire round of golf, all except the putting, without taking a step. You make a drive—that's off the first tee, you tell yourself. It hooks a little; you'd be on the left edge of the fairway; now you've got to lift a 4-iron over a long sand trap to hit the green. You push the 4-iron a little to the right; that leaves you a 20-yard pitch-and-run. So you get out the pitching wedge and try it.

I especially love to practice right at the start of the year, after the Christmas holidays. Christmas is the happiest time of the year for the professional golfer as a family man, but the worst time of year for the golfer as an athlete. Everybody eats too much at Christmas, sits around too much, gets too fat, happy and lazy. I know that the first time I pick up a club again the edge will be gone from my game, yet some of the big tournaments are coming up very soon: the Los Angeles Open, the Bing Crosby Tournament at Pebble Beach, the San Francisco Open. So it's off to the practice range, and to work.

I head somewhere where the weather is warm and the sun will beat down and soak into my muscles: I go to Palm Springs or to Arizona or to Florida. There's always a beautiful spot waiting somewhere, with good grassy tee areas to hit from and long wide fairways to aim at. The grass feels good under my spikes. The air feels good against my face. The fairway ahead is a beautiful green challenge.

In the morning I hit one hundred balls or more, taking my time, stopping to analyze every shot after I make it. Then I have lunch and hit one hundred more. Afterward, if I feel like it, I play a few holes, until I get tired. Within a single delightful week, I always have the feeling that all the mincemeat pie is out of my system and the kinks out of my muscles. It takes tournaments to put the final edge on a professional's game, but a week at the practice tee can do all but the final honing.

And what a pleasant way to spend a week! Or for that matter a single half hour, or some time every afternoon when you pass that driving range on your way home from work.

You have to have the right conditions, of course, or all the fun goes out of it. There's no pleasure in practicing when you're tired, or have something else on your mind, or when the weather's too hot or too cold, or when a stiff wind is throwing you off-balance. Hitting as many as fifty balls, one after the other, is hard physical work. It brings the sweat out on your forehead. It makes you tired. But if the circumstances are right, what a wonderful way to get tired. Your other problems are forgotten. Your muscles get that happy, relaxed, blissfully fatigued feeling that comes from doing a good job naturally and well.

As a fellow golfer, I can wish you nothing better than a good, well-built, well-kept practice tee—with good rich grass where the ball can sit down just as it does out on the course, and with big green expanses of turf stretching out in front of you. I hope that nobody ever again builds a golf course without a first-rate practice range. I hope that all the proprietors of public driving ranges put in beautifully sodded tees. For practice can be a joy, and every golfer can practice oftener than he can play. You don't have to devote a half day to practice, as you do to a round of golf. You don't have to plan it in advance and get up a foursome and set a starting time. You can practice when you feel like it, and stop whenever you choose.

Will it improve your game? Of course it will.

Golf, you see, is a very strange sport. The tennis player, even if he contents himself with a single set, hits the ball a couple of hundred times; in a three-set match he may well hit it over a thousand times. The average golfer, in the course of an eighteen-hole round, hits the ball only about forty or fifty times. The rest of his strokes are chips and putts, which involve a different technique entirely. A golfer who plays once a week for six months of the year and never practices, swings at the ball no oftener in the course of an entire year than does the tennis player in a single good match.

Small wonder that he never gets comfortable, never gets relaxed, never has that feeling of confidence that comes from constant repetition.

48

The movements involved in the golf swing, as I have tried to emphasize, are perfectly natural ones. They come easy. They require very little conscious thought. But they have to be exercised; they have to be repeated; they have to be kept free and relaxed. A man who has been in a sickbed for a long time has difficulty even in walking the first time he tries it again. The most efficient typist makes errors on her first day back from a long vacation. No kind of physical activity survives intact after a prolonged period of disuse. And it is when our bodies fail to perform their tasks automatically, without effort, that we begin thinking, try to substitute conscious control for what should be reflex action—and get into trouble. You can't think your way to walking, typing or playing golf. You get to doing it well by doing it.

But there's a right way to practice and a wrong way. Let's take a look at the average beginner as he parks his car at a driving range:

He steps right up to the counter and buys the king sized bucket of balls, to save money. Wrong! He may find that his muscles are too stiff to swing easily. Or after hitting a few balls he may find that he's not in the right mood for practice. But as long as he's invested so much, he's going to keep hitting just to get his money's worth—and he's going home a worse player than before and a man who has come to hate the very thought of practice.

He borrows a club because he doesn't have his own clubs in his car. Wrong! You practice in order to learn to swing your own clubs easily and naturally. The swing is largely a matter of *feel*. It doesn't do any good to get the feel of a club you'll never use again.

He drives off the rubber mats. Wrong! This is totally artificial. You can hit 6 inches behind the ball but bounce off the rubber and get away a pretty fair shot, thus misleading yourself entirely. It is especially wrong to hit iron shots off the rubber mats and the high tees they have—yet you see people do it all the time.

He doesn't aim at anything. He just beats the ball. If he hits a good shot, he hastens to hit another ball quickly before he forgets the secret. If he hits a bad one, he steps back frowning and wondering what went wrong—but not really thinking and analyzing. Before long, he's hitting them all badly. He's baffled and discouraged. He can't imagine what went wrong, but any pro could tell him. *Everything* has gone wrong. He's off-balance at the address. His waggle is

49

nervous and jerky. He's picking the club up with his wrists. His head is moving. He is practicing the very movements that ruin a golf shot.

Wrong, all wrong!

You've got to have your own clubs and a good grassy tee. You've got to take your time. You have to check your grip and remind yourself of the fundamentals. And you have to plan your shot; you have to pick out a spot and aim at it.

If the shot goes bad, you have to think about it. What did you do that you shouldn't have done? Did you fail to get over the ball at the address? Did you move your head? Did you forget to keep the swing compact, let the club get away from you and loosen your grip?

You have to try little adjustments and see if they help. Maybe you should shorten your backswing. Maybe you should slow down a little. Maybe you'd better recheck your grip. Maybe you'd better concentrate for a while on holding your head steady.

If you keep thinking and analyzing on the practice tee, you'll discover what's wrong. (If you can't, then the only logical next step is to consult a pro.) You'll be able to correct it.

All right, now you've got it working. You're hitting them long and straight. This is the time to relax, enjoy yourself and get that swing grooved into your habit patterns. Golf practice is not at all like a session with the barbells, where you are merely trying to build muscles. It is an attempt to develop a smooth and delightful flow of coordination. It is an attempt to wield hands, wrists, arms, body and legs into such a naturally rhythmic unity that they will perform the golf swing without thought and without effort, time after time, so that you can concentrate on the finer points of the game.

Once you've reached this stage on the practice tee, you can try some experiments. Try to find out just how much you're capable of doing. Remember the twelfth hole at your course, with those trees on the left side of the fairway, scaring you away from the best place to put your drive for a clear approach shot? In a match, you wouldn't dare risk it—but why not find out, here on the practice tee, if you could aim the ball to the left and put a little fade on it that would keep it out of trouble? And remember that dogleg to the left on the seventeenth? Why not find out if you can develop a controlled hook that will carry you around it?

You'll never know unless you try, and the practice tee is the place to find out.

Give yourself a chance. You may be pleasantly surprised to discover that you're a better golfer than you ever realized. Then keep practicing, and surprise yourself some more.

CHAPTER VI

DEVELOPING THE WINNING FRAME OF MIND

WE'RE FINISHED NOW with the fundamentals. Regardless of what you may have read elsewhere or what anyone else may have told you, that's all there is to it. If you use the correct grip, if you anchor your feet and especially your head, if you keep your swing compact—and if you practice these things until they become second nature—then you've got the mechanical side of golf licked. There's nothing in the world now to stop you from becoming a good golfer, maybe even a great golfer.

But we've still—remember those words of my father?—got 90 per cent of the game to go. We've arrived at the most important part of the game, the most interesting, the most inspiring, the part that really separates the men from the boys. We're finished with the checkers and ready to start on the chess. We will discuss, in the rest of the book, how to play golf from the shoulders up.

Golf takes more mental energy, more concentration, more determination than any other sport ever invented. It's not a team sport, where the other fellows can bail you out if you have a lapse. It's not a head-to-head contest like tennis, where you can hope that your opponent will make a mistake before you make one. It's just you and a club and a ball, trying to dominate a course that sits there like a mountain to be climbed or a river to be swum—a course that plays no favorites and shows no mercy. If you make a careless move, the course will swallow you up. To win, you have to hit every shot to the maximum of your capabilities, from first drive to final putt. You can't afford a single lackadaisical swing. You can't afford a mistake.

I'm going to talk here about how it feels to play in a tournament; you will see for yourself how the same thing applies to any golfer.

To win a tournament, you have to hit the ball harder than your opponents: you have to have power. You have to hit it straighter: in other words, you need precision. While you need power and precision to win at any sport, note how strange are the circumstances under which you have to apply them in golf.

A single round of golf lasts four long hours. A tournament, which goes on for four days, seems almost endless. Yet while playing that round or that tournament, there are very few times that you are called upon to act. There are long intervals between tee shot and approach shot, between approach and chip, between chip and putt. In a tournament there are the long waits between one day's round and the next.

The game calls for top physical effort, yet is played at low physical tension. You don't get fired up and full of adrenalin like a football player or a boxer. As a matter of fact, it would be fatal to get too fired up. A boxer who gets angry usually boxes better, unless he loses his head entirely; but a golfer who gets angry is bound to play worse.

There's no way to release the tensions that you acquire. Golf is not like football, where the physical collisions help you let off steam. In football, you can be a little mad at yourself for dropping a pass or missing a tackle, and then the next instant somebody barrels into you and knocks the memory right out of your mind; you find mental relief in the physical clash of combat. In golf there are no safety valves at all. You're under pressure; you're under tension; in a tournament you can feel the crowd's excitement and tension, which add to your own. Yet you have to execute every shot in cold blood, so to speak. You have to force yourself, each time you address the ball, to be calm and cool and detached, like a surgeon wielding a scalpel.

Strange things can happen in tournaments to add to your mental problems. In the Masters of 1958 I hit a shot on the twelfth hole of the final round which landed in a muddy bank and bored in so deep that it was totally buried. I was sure that under the rules I was entitled to lift and drop it, without penalty, but the first ruling was that I had to play the ball where it lay. If so, I was knocked out of my chance to win. I played the ball where it lay and also played a provisional ball while we waited for the final official decision. The higher ruling, which was in my favor, did not arrive until two holes later. Had I not been able to control my emotions and go ahead as if nothing had happened, I would probably have shot myself out of first place by that time—but I held onto myself and I won.

In the Phoenix tournament of 1963, two strange things happened. One involved the famous bee that chose to explore my ball as it lay on the sixth green and moved the ball a fraction of an inch as it took off again. As in the 1958 Masters, there was a long wait until I could be sure that the final official ruling would not penalize me. The other irritation was described in most newspapers as a girl's giggle which threw me off on the thirteenth green and caused me to three-putt. Actually the disturbance did not involve a girl, and I wasn't thrown off because of irritation. What happened was that two men, who obviously had drunk one or two too many, tried to leap across a ditch while I was addressing my putt, and one of them fell in, creating a scene at which everybody in the vicinity could not help laughing. I had to laugh myself when I saw what had happened and that moment, in which my mind was taken off my game, was just enough to spoil my concentration and make me miss my putt. I was a little angry afterward when I realized what the man's fall into the ditch had cost me—but not angry enough to stop myself from going on to win the tournament.

The weather can bother you—if you let it. One year in the Masters I was driving off the tenth tee, with a stiff wind blowing into my face. I was just about to swing when I felt a sudden lull in the wind. Trying to hurry and take advantage of it, I duck-hooked my ball into the woods. I could have blamed the bad shot on fate and been upset the rest of the day. Actually, analyzing what had happened, I was more irritated with myself than with the elements. Had I been concentrating fully, had I been comfortable and well set over the ball, the lull in the wind would never have thrown me off. If anything, I would merely have stepped back and got myself set again. The wind had played a part, but it was my own mistake and I resolved never to repeat it.

The course itself can get you mad—if you let it. For the British Open of 1962, the course at Troon was too unpredictable. There had been a long drought and the fairways were baked into iron. And

Troon is so full of ridges and humps that there was absolutely no telling, with the ground as hard as it was, where any shot would end up. One day, on the fifteenth, I hit what I think was probably the finest drive of my life, long and absolutely square, right down the center of the fairway on the exact line I had planned as the maximum protection against trouble. Yet when I got to the ball I found that it had bounced all the way off the fairway and into a thick tangle of downhill rough—as nasty a lie as anybody ever suffered for a roundhouse slice or horrible hook.

Things like this can bother you, all right, but you don't have to let them get you really down. When I played my first practice round over Troon, I decided right then and there that I wasn't going to let myself get locked into a life-and-death struggle with the course. Sure, it was too baked. Sure, I was going to get some bad bounces. But nobody had planned the drought; nobody was to blame. And the course was as baked for the other players as for me; everybody else was going to get bad bounces, too. I decided that I would keep the ball right in the center, as nearly as I could, to allow a maximum leeway for a bounce to either side. I decided that when I had to, I would skid the ball toward those hard greens, rather than pitch for them.

The twelfth hole at Troon was a particular monster; it is ordinarily a par 5, but for the tournament it had been converted into a terrifying 460-yard par 4. Some of the players took one look at it and threw up their hands. I myself decided to treat it with respect, but not with fear. In my own mind, I would regard it as a sort of par 4½. I would play it to take a 5 if necessary, and sort of hope for a 4 as a bonus. Instead of using a driver off the tee, risking the heavy and almost unplayable rough that lay on either side, I used a 3-wood, and sometimes a 1-iron. This left me a difficult 1-iron or 2-iron to the green, but that was the price I had to pay for safety; and I made up my mind to pay the price cheerfully. Well, in my four cracks at No. 12 I scored a 5, two 4s and a 3. And I won the tournament.

Another thing that can bother any golfer from rankest hacker to most experienced pro is the game's total unpredictability. Baseball may be a game of inches, as they say, but golf is a game of millimeters. It requires such minute precision, such a delicate sense of touch, that no golfer in the world really knows from day to day exactly how he will play. Sometimes, after working especially hard on my drives, I've got to the point where I was able to hit one after another off the practice tee with complete accuracy; I could lay them inside a 20-foot circle, 275 yards away. I thought, "Well, this is it! I've got the drive conquered; now I can concentrate on other things." But in the next tournament I hooked and duck-hooked; I didn't hit the ball 275 yards all day and never knew where it would land. Sometimes I've had such a sure touch with the putter that it was like hitting the ball through a pipe; I found it as easy to drop the ball from 30 feet as from 2 feet. Yet in the next round I played I couldn't buy a putt.

These are the hazards of golf: the unpredictability of your own body chemistry, the rub of the green on the courses, the wind and the weather, the bee that lands on your ball or on the back of your neck while you are putting, the sudden noise while you are swinging, the whole problem of playing the game at high mental tension and low physical tension.

So to play it well you need much more than mechanical skill. You have to develop a frame of mind which will allow you to do your best regardless of the hazards, regardless of the interruptions and the bad bounces. You have to develop a philosophy of golf.

In the last analysis, you make your own breaks—in golf as in life. Sure, you'll get some bad ones. But if you can roll with your misfortunes, if you can keep calm and optimistic, you'll get some good breaks too. I got plenty of them even at Troon. I got them, I know, because I was expecting them. I told myself, "Sure, the course is unpredictable. Sure, I'm going to get some bad bounces. But I'll get some good bounces, too, to make up for it." I didn't get mad at the course and sulk through the tournament waiting for the bad luck to strike. I had the feeling that sooner or later, if I just didn't let the bad breaks upset me, Lady Luck was bound to smile.

But let me take another chapter to discuss, in detail, the kind of mental attitude that I have learned golf requires.

CHAPTER VII

RELAXATION AND CONCENTRATION . . . OR, "WAS THAT A *REAL* DOG?"

THE NEWSPAPERMEN and magazine writers who follow the golf tournaments think of me as a fast finisher; and, because so much has been written about me in these terms, I suppose the public has come to feel the same way. I'm known as a come-from-behind guy. I have the reputation of just fooling around in the early stages of a tournament, then getting down to business on the last eighteen holes.

Looking back, I have to concede that an exceptional number of tournaments have seemed to go that way. In the Los Angeles Open of 1963, I was in sixth place, five strokes behind the leader, going into the last day; yet I managed to finish on top by three strokes. In 1962 I won the Palm Springs Desert Classic by making five birdies in the final round. That same year I birdied three of the last four holes to take the Texas Open by one stroke. In 1960 I was in fifteenth place after thirty-six holes of play, but made up seven strokes on the leader in the final round to win the U.S. Open.

But, believe me, I don't do it deliberately. Nobody in his right mind would want to live so dangerously.

When I walk up to the first tee on the first day of a tournament, the only thought in my head is to play every shot as well as I can, from beginning to end. I keep in mind one of my father's pet sayings: "If you don't birdie the first hole, you can't birdie them all."

In the 1960 U.S. Open at the Cherry Hills Country Club in Denver, I was in fifteenth place after the first 36 holes. In what is considered the strongest finish in the tournament's history, I shot six birdies on the first seven holes of the final round to overtake the leader and win. Here I am on my way.

I'm playing for that birdie on the first hole, and on the second and the third. The thing is that I don't always get it: golf is that kind of game. You are bound to have holes where nothing goes right, no matter how hard you try. (Will anybody ever forget that in tournament play Sam Snead once took an 8 on a short par 4? Will I ever forget the 12 on the eighteenth hole at Los Angeles which kept me from even qualifying in 1962?) You are bound to have days when nothing goes right on any of the eighteen holes. (I've shot as high as 86 in tournament play.)

The trick when this happens is to stay serene. The whole secret of mastering the game of golf—and this applies to the beginner as well as to the pro—is to cultivate a mental approach to the game which will enable you to shrug off the bad shots, shrug off the bad days, keep patient and know in your heart that sooner or later you will be back on top.

A tournament that stands out in my memory is the National Open in Denver in 1960, which I referred to earlier. I was feeling great at the time. I never felt better when I got up in the morning, never felt more comfortable standing over the ball. Every muscle in my body was toned just right. The clubs were nice and light in my hands. I knew I could hit the ball clean out of sight in that clear mountain air.

So what happened?

In the early rounds, nothing. I was always on the verge of playing well. Some of my shots turned out so fine that I watched them in amazement as they sailed away. Yet my scores were nothing to brag about. I made a few thoughtless, careless shots that were costly. My putting was off just a touch. I felt on top of the world but all I had to show for the first three rounds was a batch of scores that might enable me to finish well up, but with virtually no chance to win.

Then, on the last day, the thing that I had been waiting for finally took place. The way I was feeling, I knew it had to happen, and it did. My putts started to fall. I had got all the careless mistakes out of my system and I made no more of them. I birdied six of the first seven holes, got a 65 for the round and won the tournament.

That's the great thing about golf. If you can just keep your confidence, if you don't let the game get you down, sooner or later everything falls into place, and you have one of those rounds that you can remember with joy all the rest of your life.

If I'm a fast finisher, it's because I'm always mentally receptive to a fast finish. I play to win, even when common sense should tell me that I no longer have a chance. Even when I have been playing at my worst, or when all the breaks have been going against me, I approach each new day, each new hole, as a glorious opportunity to get going again.

The mental approach that golf requires is a peculiar and complicated mixture of abiding confidence and patient resignation, of intense concentration and total relaxation. It is not easy to explain—it is almost something that has to exist deep down in your unconscious mind—but let me try to tell you about it.

When I was in England for the British Open of 1962, I got to talking about concentration with a British sportswriter. We were trying to put the secret of golfing concentration into words, and he began wondering if the golfer's attitude was anything like that of the late Harry Houdini, the great magician and escape artist. Houdini, as you perhaps remember, trained himself to perform all sorts of incredible physical feats. He would permit himself to be wrapped around and around with chains until no ordinary man could have moved a muscle, then thrown into a river. He had his lungs so well disciplined that he could remain under water for unbelievable periods of time, and his muscles so well disciplined that they could perform incredible feats of contortion, enabling him to slip out of the chains. He was certainly one of the most amazing men of all time.

As the British newspaperman told it, Houdini was once traveling through Europe, by rail as was the custom in those days, and found at one station that the train he planned to take was about to pull out without his baggage. To keep the train standing there until his baggage arrived, he jumped onto the tracks in front of the locomotive and grasped the rails with his hands. He expected someone to try to pull him away, so he gripped with all the power of his muscles and all the determination he could muster in his mind. When it came time to let go, after the baggage had arrived, his grip was locked so tight that it took him five minutes to release the muscles. His fingers, when he finally pulled them away, were cut and bloody.

This is one type of concentration, and for some people it works. It enabled Houdini to perform superhuman feats of strength. It is the kind of concentration that many good boxers have, and probably the men who drive in auto races. But it would never work in golf.

There are other forms of concentration. Many artists and writers like to shut themselves off from the ordinary events and rhythms of life; they work alone in a garret, not thinking about heat or cold or regular mealtimes. There are some people who think they can't do their best unless they have deliberately made themselves uncomfortable; they have to starve themselves or go too long without sleep or worry and fret until they are on the verge of shooting themselves; they seek inspiration in the same way people in the Middle Ages used to seek religious ecstasy, through self-flagellation. It's all well and good in some circumstances, I suppose. But don't try any of this in golf.

No doubt about it, the golfer has to concentrate. He can't have his mind on other matters. Many a weekend round of golf at the nation's country clubs is ruined by the intrusion of thoughts about business, about the deal that didn't come off, the harsh words the boss said, the pile of work that will be on the desk on Monday morning. Many a golfer goes astray because he and his wife had a little argument at the breakfast table, or because he was held up by a traffic jam on his way to the course. You can't play good golf if you're preoccupied with thoughts of business or how to meet your bills, or if you're emotionally upset. The golf swing is too delicate; it takes too much precision.

Let me tell you about *my* kind of concentration, and how I try to build up to it when conditions permit. It isn't quite the same thing for me, a pro who has to win to keep eating, as for the amateur who simply wants to enjoy a good, competent, soul-satisfying eighteen holes on sunny Saturday morning—but there are enough similarities to point the moral.

When I can afford to do it and the tournament is one that I desperately want to win, such as the Masters or the U.S. Open, I start getting ready at least four days in advance, sometimes even sooner. I try systematically to put everything except golf out of my mind. I don't mean that I want to shut myself away from humanity as if in a garret. In fact I'm happy that my wife understands that I don't; she never thinks of trying to help me by saying she'll bundle up the children and take them to grandmother's, so that she and the kids will be out of the way. I wouldn't want that at all, would be lost without the normal, everyday routines of life to lean against. I want to be able to concentrate, all right, but I don't want life to suddenly become something strange, different from my usual world.

I wouldn't want my wife to start babying me, either. I wouldn't want her to start shushing the children and cutting off the doorbell, or bringing me hot tea and aspirin every hour on the hour. If she seemed to be worried about me, all the concentration I am aiming for would vanish.

What my wife does do, bless her, is pretend that nothing is any different, that the tournament is still weeks away, that I have all the time in the world. But quietly, without my ever knowing it, she starts to insulate me from anything that would get in the way of my concentration. She doesn't talk to me, in those four crucial days before the tournament, about any problems. If the roof has sprung a leak or if one of the children seems to have developed a tooth cavity or if the butcher has sold her a bad cut of meat, I never hear about it—not until the tournament is over and done with and life is back to normalcy.

Without my being aware of it, without anything seeming to change, my wife sets herself up as a buffer between my concentration and the problems of ordinary life. She intercepts my telephone calls and puts through only those she knows will give me pleasure. She screens the mail and explains to our friends that we're not accepting any invitations. It isn't easy to do this, of course, and it's not really my nature. I'm a gregarious fellow by instinct. I like to have lots of people around. On the golf course, for example, the bigger the gallery the better I play.

But I know from experience that the ideal way for me to prepare for a tournament is to shut out as many things aside from golf as I can. It's best that I don't meet anybody. It's best that I don't read anything. I don't want to have to think very hard about anything at all during these days—not even golf. I get up in the morning when my brain decides to awake. I have a leisurely breakfast and hit a few balls. When I feel like quitting, I quit. If I feel like having lunch, I eat. Then I hit some more practice balls if I feel like it, or maybe start around the course. If I feel like keeping on, I play the whole eighteen. If I feel like stopping, I quit. I do it all by instinct, not thinking. I *feel* my way toward the kind of state of mind I'm seeking.

In the evening, nursing a martini along while waiting for dinner, I let my mind mosey along over the details of the day—how I was hitting the ball, how I was putting, the problem I got into on the third hole because I tried to cut the corner of a dogleg too fine, the lesson I learned about how a putt breaks on the seventh green. I'm not really thinking with my conscious mind, just letting my subconscious do the job. I may sit in silence or I may chatter away to my wife about anything that pops to my tongue.

All this time something very important is happening inside me. I hardly know how to describe it. My mind, you might say, is getting cleared out. The part of my brain that deals with all the everyday problems of setting the alarm clock and driving to the hardware store, thinking about the children and answering my mail, has nothing to do. So it stops working. It quits sending out any messages about unfinished business or unanswered problems that might worry me, tighten my stomach or tense my muscles.

I read these words to my wife just now and she laughed at me. She said I sounded like a beachcomber, a bum. I don't mean that she thought so—she thought that you the reader might think so.

It isn't that at all. Ordinarily I'm one of the busiest people you ever saw. I love hustle and bustle. But if I'm going to concentrate on an important golf tournament in the way that I know is best for me, I have to do it the way I've been saying. I'm seeking what I guess you would call peace of mind. I deliberately set the process in motion by sweeping everything else out of my brain. Then, gradually, as the days before the tournament pass, the feeling seeps down into my subconscious (or unconscious) mind; it seeps all the way down into my bones.

I feel *right*. I don't know why I feel this way. I couldn't possibly describe to you exactly what it is that I feel right about, but I feel *right*. I feel ready for the tournament. I know that I can concentrate on golf no matter what happens.

I'm at peace with the world. I know I'm going to play my best.

Once a big tournament is over, Winnie and I can return happily to normalcy, particularly if I happen to have won.

Maybe I'll miss a shot—it happens to everybody—but if so I'll not be upset. Maybe an almost perfect putt will stop one grass blade away from dropping into the hole. Maybe I'll get a bad bounce on a drive and find myself in some impossible rough. Maybe I'll find myself so far behind the leaders on the last morning of the tournament that it would take a miracle to let me win. So what? I'm doing my best. I'm with it. If my luck wants to turn, I'm ready.

I'm not forcing myself to concentrate the way Houdini forced the muscles of his fingers to tighten on those rails. That kind of concentration, that kind of tension, would be fatal to a good game of golf. I'm not trying to force myself like the man in the garret, or the man in the hairshirt. I don't seek any kind of artificial, enforced concentration. I'm not trying to repress my natural instincts.

To me concentration means a total and forward-looking relationship between the mind and the challenge. The secret of that relationship is not tension but relaxation, something not tight and restrictive but free and easy, not destructive but creative, not the throttling of instincts but the release. When I concentrate on golf in those days before the tournament, I am trying to rediscover my personal resources, regroup them and match them to the challenge of the game.

At the opening tee I am ready. I know that I have the relaxed confidence that comes from my kind of concentration. I am not going to let a bad swing upset me. I am not going to moan over a bad bounce. If somebody talks while I'm putting, I'm not going to stalk off the course in anger.

If you're in a mood to be irritated, if you're touchy and full of easily injured pride, there are dozens of things in every tournament that can throw you. (And in every round of golf the amateur plays, also.) Maybe the man you are paired with likes to play faster than you do, and you have the feeling he's always pushing you to hurry your shots. Or maybe he plays so slowly that you have to wait what seems like an eternity between each shot.

All you can do is reach down into that inner layer of concentration and tolerance and roll along with the circumstances. If you start thinking irritated thoughts, the annoyance jabs down into your subconscious mind, and then it bites down through your spinal column into your stomach and your muscles. All your carefully assembled nervous and muscular coordination starts falling apart, from the inside out. Before you know it, you can't hit the ball at all.

I don't mean that, feeling serene, you can walk around the course like a saint, totally oblivious to annoyance. Naturally you will enjoy the game more with a congenial partner than with an uncongenial one. You will be happier when the ball takes a lucky bounce than when it skids off into the rough. You will feel better when you're a stroke up than when you're a stroke down. But if you've built the right mental attitude, you can live with anything.

Do you remember the old story about the putter and the dog? Four good golfing friends had made a one-week trip to an expensive winter resort, with the understanding that the high man at the end of the week would pay the bill. They finished the week all even and decided to stay another day for another eighteen holes. They were still even after this eighteen, and after the next, day after day while the bills kept mounting up. Eventually there came a day when, on the eighteenth green, one of the men had to sink a tough, downhill, 40-foot putt or be the loser.

He lined it up carefully, said a little prayer and started his back-swing. At that moment a dog suddenly appeared over a bunker and trotted across the green, right over the line of the putt. Without even hesitating in his swing, the man hit the ball. It curled neatly and dropped in. His friends were so amazed that they were speechless until long after they had all had their showers. Then one of them finally said, "I want to tell you that the way you sank that putt, after that dog walked across the green, was the greatest display of coolness and courage I've ever seen on a golf course."

"Good Lord!" cried the man who had sunk the putt. "Was that a *real* dog?"

In its own tongue-in-cheek way, this story says exactly what I've been trying to say. In every round of golf, problems are going to arise. Some of them will be real; some of them will just be in your head. You have to be prepared to cope with all of them, the real and the imagined. You have to develop the mental approach which will always insure that you will never beat yourself: if you lose, it must be only because the other man played better.

Once you have acquired this mental attitude, miracles can happen. They are bound to happen.

They have happened to me often in tournaments. Or in matches, which are in a way even more difficult because you keep watching your opponent face to face. Let's say the match has gone twelve or thirteen holes. I'm not driving as far or as straight as usual and my

putts have not been dropping. I'm two holes down and am lucky it's not worse; I'm not getting any better and my opponent is playing like a machine.

The gallery thinks I've had it for the day. *I* know I may have had it, I can't help facing the fact that I'm probably going to lose. But I know then what I must do. I'm below my peak because I don't feel right inside myself. I've let some tension creep in. I've got to reach down inside myself and recover that feeling of total peace of mind. I've got to concentrate the way a golfer is meant to concentrate, in that relaxed, free and easy way that will let the swing *flow*.

When I succeed, the miracle often happens. The club feels better, lighter. I hit a beauty off the tee and sink a lucky putt. Suddenly I'm only one down and the gallery is roaring, and I know at that moment that I can't help winning.

Next day, often as not, the newspapers will say that I pulled myself together at the fourteenth hole and got a grip on myself; I forced myself to make a superhuman effort and made an impossible comeback. Actually it was just the opposite. I had been trying too hard up to the fourteenth hole, and then I relaxed. A dog could have walked across the line of my putts and I would hardly have noticed.

Now then. I have been talking about how *I* feel. How does all this apply to the amateur golfer?

It applies right down the line. If you are to play your best game, you have to develop this same kind of mental attitude; you have to be relaxed and concentrated at the same time, confident and patient.

No, you can't devote four days or a week to preparing for your Saturday round. You can't indulge yourself in that lazy-daisy beachcomber's life that I find so helpful. I myself can't afford to do it very often.

You may not even be able to start concentrating on golf at the breakfast table. There may be some chores you have to do before you can go out to the course. There may be some decisions to make. One of the children may skin a knee or the neighbor's dog may start rooting up your flower beds. There are all kinds of things that can get in the way.

But at least you can do this: the minute you leave for the course, you can put your problems out of your mind and start thinking

70

nothing but golf thoughts. You can use the ten minutes or half hour that it takes to get to the course to concentrate on your game. What did you do well the last time you played? What did you do badly? Remember how that drive you sent out to the left on the first hole took a big bounce on the hard turf and nearly wound up in a trap? The fairways are going to be even harder this week; so let's keep the ball to the right this time. Remember how you misread the second green? There's a lot more break on that green, for some reason, than there used to be, so allow for it this time.

Was your grip perhaps a little sloppy last time? Think about it a while. Run over the principles of the grip in your mind. They're simple enough; they don't take any deep thought. Just remind yourself of them.

It's amazing what you can do to calm yourself, clearing everything else out of your mind and concentrating on the game in just the brief span of time it takes you to get out to the course. In early 1963 I was staying near Palm Beach and had an exhibition to play in Jacksonville; so I had arranged to fly up there Sunday morning in my plane. The weather turned blustery overnight and it was cold, cloudy and windy when I took off. It wasn't the easiest kind of day to be flying and I had to work every minute of the way; when I got to the Jacksonville airport I felt tired and cranky. But, happily, somebody met me and drove me to the golf course; on the way I just closed my eyes, forgot the plane ride and thought about golf. By the time I teed off I felt fresh and eager, and I won the match.

Many players, I've noticed, talk about everything in the world except golf just before they start to play. I've ridden to the course in automobiles where all the conversation was about business problems or taxes or the state of the stock market. When that happens I try to close my ears and think my own thoughts. And I know that I'm going to beat the other fellows, even if I give them more strokes than usual, because I'm going to be a lot closer to my best game than they can possibly be to theirs.

Another thing you can do that will help immensely is approach the golf course as a friend, not an enemy. You can develop the peace of mind that comes from knowing you will do the best you can under the circumstances, the circumstances including the fact that you can't spend as much time playing golf or concentrating on it as a pro can.

The average golfer's greatest mental error, the psychological mistake that frustrates him all his life, keeping him from breaking 100 or 90 or whatever his ambition happens to be, is this: He starts off every round expecting something to go wrong. He is suspicious of his own talents. He worries.

How many times has a golfing friend turned to you, after firing three double-bogeys in a row, and begged in agonized tones, "What am I doing wrong? Forgetting to pivot? Swinging too flat?"

The minute a golfer starts talking like that—and most amateurs do, at one time or another—he's through for the day.

If you have actually acquired a fatal habit in your grip or your swing, you can't possibly discover it and correct it while you're out on the course. You won't be able to sense it yourself. Your friends, unless they are exceptionally observant, won't see it. What they tell you, if they try to tell you anything, will almost surely be wrong.

This is what club professionals are for. It takes an expert to find a flaw, though even the expert may not be able to find it right away. You'll have to go to the practice tee with him and hit a lot of balls. Sooner or later, you and he will manage to correct it.

The chances are, however, that you haven't really fallen into a fatal habit. You have simply hit a few bad balls, as anybody (including the pros) is bound to do from time to time, and let it get you down. Your confidence is shot. You're not focusing on playing the game free and easy; instead you are worrying about all those complicated and hopeless little details like the weight shift and the pivot. You're tense; your coordination is gone.

You will get it back if you can discipline your mind once more into the channels we have been discussing. If you can relax, instead of trying harder, your touch will return. Or you can get it back on the practice tee, where hitting ball after ball will release your tensions and restore your confidence.

You can't get it back by complaining to your friends or tossing your club in the air. You can't get it back by thinking about your hands, your wrists, your hips and your feet. Simmer down—or go back to the clubhouse, have a drink and a shower, and wait to try again another day, perhaps after re-reading this chapter.

CHAPTER VIII

HOW TO REACH
INSIDE YOURSELF
WHEN IN TROUBLE

THERE IS ONE IMPORTANT ASPECT of professional golf that the spectators never see, either in person or on the television screen. You can't see it but it's there, all the time, and it influences the result of every tournament. It makes the difference between a player who's consistently in the money and a player who comes up only occasionally with a big win. It's the reason that even the best of the amateurs have a hard time earning any tournament money the first year or two.

Perhaps you've run into it yourself. You belong to a nice little country club or play all your golf at a public course down the road. You've played the course for years and know it like the back of your hand. You do pretty well there, shooting a steady 80 to 85. Then some day you're invited to play at a course a hundred miles away. You know that the other men in your foursome are strictly 90 to 100 shooters; so you give them all a couple of strokes, make a couple of big Nassau bets and tee off with complete confidence. Three holes later, you suddenly realize that you're getting clobbered. Everybody in the foursome is playing better than you. At the end of the day you pay your money and go home wondering what in the world went wrong.

What happened is hardly a mystery, but it's something that most golfers never think about.

Let's say that your own course is flat—as level as a football field. The fairways aren't watered; so the ground is hard and the grass is very short and thin. You're used to tight lies, where the ball sits right down against the ground as if it were lying on a tabletop. You've been getting great distance out of your drives, which tend to travel low and get a good long roll. The greens on the course, unlike the fairways, are watered every day. You always pitch to the flag because the greens hold so well; a nice high pitch shot will always stop dead where it lands. For putting purposes, the greens are very slow. You've developed a bold, strong putting stroke to push the ball through the heavy grass.

Now, all of a sudden, just a hundred miles away, you find yourself up in the hills. The fairways go up, down and sideways. You're faced for the first time in years—perhaps for the first time in your life—with uphill, downhill and sidehill lies. The fairways are lush and those low line drives you send out from the tee won't roll. The lies you get on the fairway are deep, with the ball nestling down half its diameter into the grass. The greens, on the other hand, are close-cropped and hard. You keep sending those pitch shots up to the flag and they keep bouncing right off the back of the green. When you putt, you go way past the hole—until you start getting timid and are afraid to stroke the ball at all. You're in deep trouble because the brand of golf this course requires is almost as different from the brand you play on your own course as is baseball from football.

The next time you watch a professional tournament, I hope you'll think about this, because it will surely increase your enjoyment of what you are seeing and will help you play better golf yourself. The pros, remember, have to play all kinds of courses. At the start of the year they play in California, where the fairway grass stays alive all winter and provides very little roll. Then they go to Arizona, where the grass is dormant and you can get tremendous distance out of your drives. Next they alternate between Florida, where the grass is alive and heavy, and Louisiana and Texas, where they are back in the land of the lengthy roll. On the courses they play in the South, all the way from Florida to Texas, they seldom see a hill. In some other parts of the nation they never see a hole that is flat. They play on rye grass,

Bermuda grass, bent grass and on rye seeded over Bermuda, which is a different story entirely. They putt over greens that are as smooth and fast as billiard table and on greens where the grass is as rough and spiky as a porcupine's coat.

Just to complicate matters further, they may go abroad for tournaments and find still new sets of strange conditions. When I won the British Open at Troon in 1962, as I have mentioned, there had been a drought and the course was very hard and dry; it played something like our own Texas and Arizona courses in the winter. But I played another British course just a few miles away where the grass was as lush as it always is at Augusta for the Masters. When I toured South Africa with Gary Player that same year, I found a completely new kind of grass, something like our own Bermuda but a little coarser, and greens with the most grain I have ever seen anywhere. I was there two weeks and never did get completely adjusted, despite all my experience with the different U.S. courses.

Remember, too, that we pros almost always have to play the full course, from tees set as far back as they can possibly be stretched. For our tournaments the flags are placed at the trickiest part of the green, and then are moved next day to an even trickier spot that the chairman of the tournament has fiendishly dreamed up overnight.

Often when we are playing a course, some of the better amateurs who belong to the club walk along with us and get to wondering about our game. I've heard them say, after I've had a bad round and perhaps been a stroke or two over par, "Gosh, I believe *I* could have beaten Palmer today. Maybe *I* ought to turn pro."

Take it from a man who's been through it, it's not that easy.

When I turned pro in 1954, I *thought* it was going to be easy. I had won the National Amateur that year with considerable ease. There wasn't another amateur around whom I didn't think I could beat, day in and day out. I had played with some of the pros and I figured I could handle them, too. My greatest worry—I hate to confess this, but it's a fact—was that I would win one of the big tournaments, carrying a lot of first-place prize money, before I was entitled under P.G.A. rules to accept the money. (In those days, the rules said that an amateur who turned pro had to wait six months before he could win any money in a P.G.A. tournament.)

What a foolish worry that was! The best I could do in my first ten tournaments was finish fifth. In most of them I was out of the first ten entirely.

I hadn't realized how good the pros were. In amateur golf one man can dominate the field. I had done it, I guess, and at other times men like Jack Nicklaus and Frank Stranahan have certainly done it. You're more or less in a class by yourself. Nobody's going to come along and beat you, except once in a while and mostly by accident. But in professional golf, if there are 149 other players in the tournament, there are 149 men you have to worry about. Any one of them— even a player about whom the public has scarcely heard—can come up with his peak game and beat you in a tournament. He may beat you every time for a month, or for a whole year.

I hadn't thought about the great variety of courses on which I would have to play. I had never seen a perfectly flat course until I turned pro, and the first time I did I could hardly believe my eyes. My judgment of distance was off completely. I would figure that I was 160 yards from the flag, which is my normal 6-iron distance, hit the 6-iron perfectly and watch with utter disbelief as the ball fell 20 to 30 yards short. I also had trouble reading the new greens. The more experienced pros, who knew all about the difference that types of grass and watering conditions can make, could take one step on the fringe of the green and judge exactly how the ball would act. I had to learn all this. So does every other beginner on the tour.

You may have noticed over the years that an amateur who turns pro may do fairly well in his first few tournaments, then drop out of sight. Let's say that a California youngster turns pro and plays his first few tournaments in his home state. He gets a piece of the money every time and the newspapers play him up as the new sensation of the pro circuit. Then the tournaments start moving east and his scores start mounting. He drops right out of the money and the only place you see his name is at the bottom of the lists. The golf writers give up on him and sometimes he gives up on himself. It looks as if he had every chance, got off to a good start that should have given him confidence and then, when the chips were down in day-in-and-day-out competition, came up empty.

It's not really his fault at all. He's simply running into the harsh facts of life about professional golf. He hasn't yet learned to play on all kinds of courses in all kinds of weather. He never had to do it before so he had no opportunity to learn. Nor has he developed all the great variety of shots that it takes to win under these conditions against this kind of competition.

Up to the time I turned pro, I had always "driven" the ball. Regardless of whether I was hitting a wood off the tee or trying to send a 6-iron or even a little wedge shot to the green, I always stroked the ball hard and low. I had lots of power but very little finesse. And all around me, I suddenly realized, the more experienced pros were doing things to the ball that I had never even thought of. They knew how to make the ball stop on difficult greens by fading it in from left to right, with lots of cut on it. They knew how to send up little pitch shots that floated high in the air and dropped as gently as feathers.

I had to take stock. If I went on playing as I had always played, I might be able to make a living, but I would never get anywhere near the top. If I wanted the kind of success I had always hankered for, I had to learn everything the other pros knew. I made my choice, and spent more hours at the practice tees than I like to think about.

Besides learning new kinds of shots—in fact, even more important than that—I had to realize the full meaning of what my father had in mind when he kept saying that 90 per cent of golf is played from the shoulders up. I had to learn to think my way through every round— never doing anything automatically or out of force of habit, always surveying all the conditions, always exploring the possibility of try- ing something new and different that might work.

The next time you watch a professional play, try to put yourself inside his mind. What is he thinking? Why has he chosen that par- ticular club? Why did he hit that shot unusually high, or unusually low? What spot on the fairway or green was he aiming for? If you keep asking yourself these questions, and find the answers, your own game is bound to improve immeasurably.

Let me give you an example of the kind of mental approach to golf that distinguishes the touring professional from even the best of the amateurs. A few years ago at Palm Springs I was playing in a four- some; a good friend of mine, a fine Los Angeles amateur named Art Anderson, was my partner. We came to a hole that had a lake extend- ing into the fairway, just in front of the green, and Art hit the ball a little shorter than he intended and wound up in the water. He was barely in; the ball was barely covered.

We walked up to the lake and I saw that Art was automatically going to lift the ball and drop it. This is what most of the books of advice to young golfers tell you to do: if you get in the water, don't waste any more shots trying to get out. Remember that water refracts light and gives you a false notion of where the ball is sitting. Remember that even Lawson Little once took twelve strokes trying to get out of the water in a Greater Greensboro Open. So take your medicine. Lift the ball, drop it back, accept your one-stroke penalty and pray for better luck next time.

I have no quarrel with this advice. It's the best thing to do nine times out of ten, maybe ninety-nine times out of a hundred. But it's that other one time in ten or one in a hundred that you have to watch for.

In this case the ball was lying so shallow that there was no danger of refraction. And, anyway, under the circumstances of our match, Art Anderson had no choice. He had already taken two shots. If he lifted the ball he would lie 3—and then he still had a dangerous and difficult pitch over the water to the green. He would have to be lucky to get a double-bogey 6, and could easily take a triple-bogey 7. We were playing low ball and aggregate and if he lifted out of the water we were bound to lose the aggregate.

So I stopped him. "Come on, now," I said. "It's sitting there just as nice and big as you please. You can hit it!"

He tried it and sent the shot right to the green. He almost got his par, did get a bogey and saved the hole for us. He was as pleased as if he had just sunk a hole in one.

Something of the same sort often happens in sand traps. When the amateur gets into a fairway trap, he almost always reaches automatically for a wedge or a pitching iron; he's satisfied just to get out. But there are many sand trap lies where the ball sits up nicely, no bank stands in the way and you can safely use a long iron or even a 4-wood and knock the ball all the way up to the green. If you watched the World Golf Championship of 1964, either in person or on television, you may have seen the perfect example. On the eighteenth hole, in the third round, young Dick Sikes hit his tee shot into a fairway sand trap. He reached for an iron and took his stance, then had a second thought. Even though his ball was perilously close to the front lip of

the trap, he had an uphill lie that would help him lift the ball into the air quickly. So he went back to his bag, took out a wood and knocked the ball all the way onto the green—thus saving a stroke. This kind of thinking is one reason Sikes was such a success in his first year as a pro. Every golfer should keep his eyes and his mind open, constantly looking for such opportunities to do the unconventional.

The pro—watch him next time—is always thinking. He is thinking about the direction and speed of the wind, and the condition of the fairway. He is looking for the best spot to aim the ball, balancing the dangers of getting into a trap or the rough against the advantages of being in position for a nice open second shot to the green. He is always prepared to sacrifice the artistic for the practical. After all, the entire idea of golf is to get the ball in the hole in the fewest possible number of strokes. There is no point in sending a perfect pitch shot to the flag if the green won't hold; so the pro will gladly settle for a little punch shot and roll the ball on; it doesn't look as pretty but it gets the job done. Rather than live dangerously by pitching over a sand trap, the pro will often use a low-numbered iron or even a putter and run the ball through the trap. He is always looking for lies and grass conditions which will permit him to use his putter rather than a chip shot when he's off the edge of the green, for there is always less danger of error with the putter.

And when the pro gets in trouble—as is bound to happen to everybody from time to time—that's when you can see him at his best. When he's in deep rough, a hopeless lie, trees in the way, everything against him, that's when he reaches down inside himself for skills he doesn't even know he had. That's when he thinks most clearly how he has to swing the club; that's when he concentrates so deeply that he almost wills the ball back to safety. It's a beautiful thing to watch. If you look for it and appreciate what is going on in his mind at the time, you will find it your greatest thrill as a golfing spectator.

Note also what the pro does when he's been in trouble, has had to waste a stroke, despite a gallant try, and now finds himself almost hopelessly out of the running for a par—maybe 200 yards out from a small, tricky green with two banks of trees in front of him, and sand traps guarding the flag. Watch how often he reaches inside himself again and hits a 2-iron that you can hardly believe—straight as an arrow, right down that little lane between the trees, then hooking a little at the end, taking a big bounce, threading its way past the sand traps and finally stopping 5 feet from the pin. You can't believe it and in a way neither can he. Nobody can hit the ball that well—but *he* did because he had to. In my own career I've managed to make some clutch shots that I could never possibly have got away with if I had even for a moment entertained the idea of giving up. One that I remember particularly was on the final hole of the P.G.A. of 1964, a very close tournament in which I still had a chance to beat Bobby Nichols, who was playing just in back of me, but also was having trouble holding my tie for second place with Jack Nicklaus, who was playing along with me. The eighteenth hole was a par 5, and I figured I absolutely had to have a birdie. Unfortunately I tried too hard to reach the green with my second shot, overswung, hooked and wound up right on a macadam roadway between two rows of trees, off to the left of the green. There I was with an almost impossible third shot—and, to make matters worse, Jack Nicklaus had put his second shot right on the green and was almost sure to get an easy birdie. It was going to take a miracle to save me, so the only thing to do was make a miracle. I used a 5-iron, choking up on it, punched the ball out through the trees, hit short of the green, just where I had to land, and rolled up close enough to get down in one putt. That was the day that Bobby Nichols refused to make a single mistake and beat me anyway, but at least I held my tie for second.

Later in '64 came the World Championship, with its two hundred thousand dollars' prize money, the most that had ever been offered in a single tournament. Again on the eighteenth hole of the final round, I desperately needed a birdie to retain my chance of winning the tournament from Bobby Nichols, who again was playing just behind me, and to save second place from Gary Player, who was playing along with me. Both Gary and I tried hard off the tee of this par 4. Gary tried so hard that he landed deep in the rough, but fortunately I got away with my swing and sent out one of the finest drives I have ever hit in my life. Walking down the fairway, I figured that without doubt I had Gary beaten and that I might even win the whole thing.

Then I saw my lie. The ball had rolled just a little too far; it lay right at the edge of the fairway, smack against the heavy rough and in fact a little under the overhanging edge of the rough. The chances of getting the ball out of there and making it stop on the green—or for that matter anywhere near the green—looked like about one in a hundred. Again, to make matters worse, Gary Player did the impossible and put his second shot on the green.

Well, I could have cursed my luck and merely slashed at the ball, just to get it away from that horrible lie. Instead I said, "Okay, let's see if we can't get a birdie from here, which would be considerably more of an accomplishment than getting a birdie from the tee." I used a 6-iron and cut under the ball, right through the heavy grass, faded the shot in from left to right and hit the pin. I knew right then that nothing could stop me from sinking that putt for a birdie, and so did Gary; walking down the fairway, he shook his head in mock despair. As it happened, Bobby Nichols beat me again that day, but at least I had second place and the immense satisfaction of having made a shot that couldn't be made.

Most amateurs give up too quickly when they get in trouble on the golf course. Take a businessman who's out there; he's playing against some friends who are also arch rivals; he doesn't care about that fifty-cent Nassau he's got going, but he wants more than anything to beat those friendly enemies of his, just to show them. He hooks his tee shot into the deep rough, while everybody else in the foursome gets out far and straight on the fairway, and immediately he gives up on the hole. All he tries to do is pitch the ball out of the rough, then aim his third shot more or less in the direction of the green. He's decided he's already lost this one—so why kill himself?

If that same businessman were faced with ruin at the office, you'd never catch him taking his bad luck lying down. He'd grit his teeth and start thinking. He would concentrate so hard that he wouldn't know it was lunchtime, wouldn't know it if an earthquake shook his desk. Sooner or later, he'd come up with a solution. One way or another, he'd weather the crisis and save the business.

Why not at golf?

Try it. Start thinking your way around the course, calculating the risks and advantages of every possible kind of shot. Ask yourself if you can get away with a 4-wood out of that trap, instead of settling for a little iron shot. Ask yourself if you hadn't better run the ball up to the green, instead of pitching it. And when you get in trouble, reach inside yourself. You'll probably find more there than you ever knew existed.

Sometimes, of course, you'll fail—miserably. (The pros do, too.) Maybe you'll fail most of the time. But until you've dared to try and have brought off an impossible shot from the rough or from the water, or have salvaged a hole by laying a monster of a 2-iron shot stiff against the pin, you will have missed golf's greatest playing thrill.

I've told many businessmen golfers, in person, the things I have been saying in this chapter. And sometimes I've run into a reaction that you may also have at this point. "I just don't want to play the game that hard," the amateur will say. "I'm playing for fun and relaxation. I don't want to make a federal case out of it."

Well, now, wait a minute.

Sure, the amateur plays for fun. The question is: How can he have the most fun? Only, in my opinion, by playing the game to the hilt. If all you're doing is walking around the course and swinging the club aimlessly, without thought and without concentration, you may as well be taking a walk in the woods, which is cheaper and will give you an equal amount of exercise. But if you're playing golf as a sport—and I'm convinced that most people play it as a sport, not just for the exercise, as is proved by the recent popularity of golf carts which take most of the exercise out of it—you have to play to win in order to enjoy it.

You want to have fun. You want to relax and get away from your business woes, your personal problems, the tensions of everyday life. The way to do it is to concentrate on the game, to think about golf and nothing but golf. Your four hours on the course should take you into a different world, where you are totally absorbed in a form of thinking, action and strategy completely different from anything you do the rest of the week. That's the way to get the utmost in pleasure and energy-restoring refreshment out of golf. The harder you work at the game, the more it will relax you.

Lots of people work as hard at their hobbies as at their jobs. Painting takes intense concentration. So does photography, if you want to do it well. The man with a woodworking shop in his basement combines mental and physical effort of the most exacting kind. Yet these people all find something in their hobbies that takes them out of their routine, recharges their batteries, and sends them back to work next day bright-eyed and eager.

If the kind of concentration you apply on the golf course is the Houdini kind, I'll grant that playing the game will exhaust you. You can't maintain that kind of muscle-tensing, teeth-gritting concentration for four hours without paying the penalty. But we're not talking about the Houdini brand of do-or-die effort. We're talking about a different kind of concentration, one which recognizes that golf is still just a game, but a game worthy of the utmost respect and attention.

A bad round, I'll grant, will also exhaust you. There's something about hitting your shots badly, fighting the rough and struggling out of sand traps that wears the muscles down and stamps fatigue into every cell of your body. And you'll have days like that, no doubt about it. But even this is good for your soul. It's a different kind of fatigue from the kind you get on the job. You go home worn out, but in a way you never feel in your everyday life. Next day you wake up feeling like a new man, totally refreshed, ready for whatever the week may bring. It does a person good, in this sedentary society of ours, to get physically exhausted once in a while.

So play golf to the hilt. Win, lose or draw, good day or bad, you'll be happier for it and you'll live longer.

CHAPTER IX

THE NEGLECTED
ART OF USING
THE RIGHT CLUB

You could make a pretty good living standing near any green at any country club or public course in America and betting even money that the next approach shot you saw would be short of hole high. Watch it the next time you play. Most golfers are consistently short of the pin, even short of the green. The majority of approach shots hit by the average golfer are far too weak. Hardly ever does the average golfer go over the green.

This has to mean that most golfers use the wrong club most of the time. They're using a 4-iron when they should use a 3-iron and a 7-iron when they should use a 6- or even a 5-iron.

Why do you suppose they do this?

Because most golfers *think* they hit the ball a lot farther than they *actually do*.

Maybe it comes from watching the pros. I myself average about 185 yards with a 3-iron, 165 yards with a 5-iron, and 140 yards or more with a 7-iron—and I don't try to hit the ball at full strength with my irons. Perhaps the average golfer, after watching a pro drop a 5-iron shot right next to the pin from 165 yards out, thinks that he's supposed to do it, too.

Or perhaps it comes from the tables of distance you see in so many golf books. The tables say that you're supposed to hit a 9-iron 120 yards, and get 10 yards more each time you move to a longer club—in other words 130 yards with an 8-iron, 160 yards with a 5-iron, and 180 yards with a 3-iron. The figures are probably all right, on the average. If you measured iron shots by one thousand fairly good players and took the average, you'd probably come out with that kind of result. But it's another of those cases like the old story about the six-foot man who drowned trying to walk across a river he had been told averaged five feet deep.

Some players, without straining, can easily hit a 5-iron 165 yards. Others, even if they swing as hard as they can, will never get more than 140 yards out of a 5-iron. Many women players barely get 120 yards.

Since so many players under-club themselves on all their approach shots, I'm almost tempted to say that you can knock five strokes a round off your game simply by using one club longer than you think you should use—in other words, by reaching for a 3-iron every time you think you should use a 4-iron, and for the 7-iron every time you should use an 8-iron. Perhaps you should try this sometime, just for fun. But this would be too simple; it would be another easy but fallacious guide, like those distance tables you see printed.

What you really should do, if you want to improve your approaches, is make up your own table of distances. And you can only do this through constant practice and observation. Keep a record of your iron shots. How far do you *really* hit a 3-iron? How much distance do you *really* average with a 7-iron? Find out, and then abandon any notions of false pride. There's not much advantage, when you get right down to it, in being able to hit a 7-iron farther than anybody else at your course. The irons are accuracy clubs, not distance clubs. If you have to use a 5-iron to reach a green that your best friend—who stands two inches taller and weights thirty more pounds—can reach with a 6-iron, so what? The idea is to get there, with whatever tool will do the job best.

If you keep tab on the distance you can reasonably expect to get out of your clubs, you'll soon discover something else that every pro knows. The distance never stays quite the same from day to day. When you're feeling strong and everything is going right for you, the distance goes up. When you're not quite feeling your best, the distance goes down.

The Neglected Art of Using the Right Club

I've played the Latrobe Country Club more often than any other course in America—thousands of times, I guess—and naturally a lot of my tee shots have landed in more or less the same general area. But I don't always use the same iron for my second shot. Even if I played the same course every day and every tee shot landed in the exact same spot, I'd switch irons from time to time, depending on how I felt. Some days, when the club felt nice and light in my hands, I might use a 5-iron. The next day I might use a 4-iron, even a 3-iron.

The wind is a factor. There's one hole at Pebble Beach, as you've probably heard, where you can reach the green from the tee with an 8-iron when those seaside gales are with you, and have to get out the driver when the wind is against you. But it's more than the wind. It's *you*. Maybe you *average* 160 yards with a 5-iron—but on days when you're at the peak of your game you'll hit it 170 yards, and on other days you'll hit it only 145 yards.

You can't be stubborn when it comes to reaching for a club. You can't say to yourself, "I'm 150 yards out, the golf books say a 6-iron should travel 150 yards, so I'll reach for a 6"—even though you've never hit a 6-iron shot that far in your life. You can't even say, "I'm 150 yards out. I know from long experience and observation that I average 150 yards with my 6-iron, so I'll reach for a 6"—even though on this particular day your irons have all been falling short. You have to think about your past experience and your present body chemistry, both things, and then do what logic dictates. It's just another part of playing golf from the shoulders up.

What kind of clubs should you carry in your bag? Again, it's a matter of individuality. Some pros—amateurs, too—are great with a 4-wood; they couldn't play their best without it. Some players even like to carry a 5-wood, rather than some of the middle irons.

I myself usually have only two woods in my bag: a driver for off the tee and a 3-wood for all long fairway shots. I carry all the irons from the No. 1, with which I average around 225 yards, to the No. 9, with which I average around 115 yards. And I also carry a sand wedge and a pitching wedge. My putter, of course, makes the four-teenth club.

Let me tell you about the pitching wedge. I suppose that the great majority of amateurs don't even own one—but it's in many ways the greatest golf club ever invented and you need it to play your best.

Almost every pro in the business uses the pitching wedge on almost every shot from about 100 yards on in. A full swing with the wedge will send the ball high in the air for around 100 yards and stop it dead where it lands on the green. By shortening your backswing, you can get great accuracy from 80 yards or from 50 yards—any distance at all.

If you open the face of the wedge, you can send the ball almost straight up; you can clear a fifty-foot tree that stands right in front of you and stop it dead just on the other side. You can pitch and run with the wedge. Or, if you close the face and hit down sharply, you can send out a little liner that looks as if it would roll forever, but has so much backspin that it bites right into the green and stops as if it had brakes.

It's not an easy club to use. You'll have to practice with it a great deal before you master it. You may find that it's particularly difficult to use from a tight lie, because you have to stroke the ball very accurately with the clubface; any tendency to look up, to peek before you have completed the shot, can be fatal. But once you've mastered the wedge, it's great. Most pros use it in even the tightest lies out of the thinnest grass. It was a wedge shot that I sank, from a tight and nasty lie, on the sixteenth hole at Augusta in 1962, for the birdie that I needed in order to go on and win.

Whatever other clubs you decide to carry, do yourself a favor and include a pitching wedge. Some players get along nicely without a driver; they find they can average a little more distance off the tees with the shorter but safer 2-wood. Some players get along without a wood to use on the fairways; they do all right with a 1-iron or 2-iron. Lots of players would never think of carrying a 1-iron, which seems to pose some special difficulties—though I think most of them are psychological—for the average golfer. But no pro would think of playing without a pitching wedge in his bag, and you shouldn't think about it, either—for the wedge is the greatest stroke-saver golf has ever known.

CHAPTER X

HOW TO BUY A SET OF CLUBS AND THE RIGHT BALL FOR YOU

IF YOU'VE JUST DECIDED this very second to take up golf and have an irresistible urge to rush right now to the nearest sporting goods counter and buy a set of clubs, let me give you one word of advice.

Don't!

Buying a set of clubs isn't something to be done casually and on the spur of the moment, like buying a new tie. It's more like getting married. It's a long-term deal and an important one; it may be the major factor in determining how happy or unhappy you are every Saturday and Sunday for the next five years. It's also a big investment because a good set of four woods, eight irons, a pitching wedge and a putter will cost you a couple of hundred dollars.

Let's talk for a moment about clubs.

As you probably know, I'm in the club manufacturing business. But I'm not going to try to tell you that nobody but the Arnold Palmer Company makes good clubs. I have a great deal of respect for all the top-flight manufacturers. They have all put a great deal of time and money into the study of golf clubs. The pros who work for them are constantly trying out new ideas for them: different kinds of shafts, new materials, new angles for the clubheads, new weight balances. I spend a lot of time on the practice tee with a roll of lead tape in my pocket; I'll try a piece of tape near the toe of a driver, adding a fraction of an ounce of weight, then shift the tape to the heel area, back and forth, looking for the spot where the extra weight may help.

One reason you see better golf scores today than ever before is the equipment, for there is simply no comparison between today's golf clubs and the old wood-shafted clubs that were in style until the mid-thirties. Those wood-shafted clubs took tremendous skill to handle. There was a lot of torque in that wood; you could hold the grip in one hand and with your other hand twist the clubhead almost to a right angle. Every time our grandfathers took a backswing the head twisted around a little, and on the downswing it had to twist back. That is, they *hoped* it would twist back to its original angle. Often it didn't and the shot was spoiled.

Wooden shafts were also subject to fatigue. Every time our grandfathers hit the ball, the shaft weakened a little and grew more flexible; a club that was just right the day it was bought was soon a different club entirely. At a country club in Scotland I once saw the racks where the old Scottish golfers used to put their clubs for a rest. The theory was that if you stored the clubs for a time, in a position that kept them from warping, the shafts would regain their original strength. I doubt very much that this actually happened—though it probably helped the golfers' psychology.

Today, no matter what brand of clubs you buy, they'll be the best that modern materials and modern engineering can produce, and they'll be beauties. The shafts will be made of finest steel and probably tapered in sections to give added protection against torque. The clubheads will be set on at the best possible angle to produce on-line shots, and the grooves will be deep and sharp to give backspin to the ball and help it bore a straight path.

Take a look some time at the face of any good driver. Notice the bulge in it? That's a clever little invention which helps far more than most golfers realize to make up for any error in the swing. If every golfer caught the ball in the exact center of the clubface every time, that bulge wouldn't be necessary. But no golfer is that perfect; all of us keep catching the ball at a spot a little toward the shaft, or a little toward the toe. If the clubhead were perfectly flat, a ball caught on the shaft side of center would always slice and a ball caught toward the toe would always hook. The slight surface angle provided by the bulge is just enough to counteract this kind of error and bring the ball back to a straight line. You have to make a *big* error nowadays to hook or slice a drive badly.

You'd be surprised how many things like this the manufacturers know about you the golfer. They know that if you are like the great majority of players, you have a tendency to slice the ball a little every time; so they build most of their clubs with the heads set at a slight angle to counteract a slice. But they also know that a substantial minority of golfers tends to hook the ball every time; so they also build clubs with the heads set to correct for a hook. They provide extra stiff shafts—X shafts—for the pros who are strong enough to generate all their own power. They also make a standard stiff or S shaft, and a regular or R shaft which is much whippier, to help the average player get more speed with the clubhead in the hitting area. They also make X, S and R shafts for women.

Whatever kind of physique you have, whatever the strength or weakness of your wrists and shoulders, whatever your natural style of swing, there is almost surely a set of clubs waiting on the racks that would suit you. Even if you happen to be the one player in a hundred who needs something special—such as extra-long clubs for the man with short arms—you can have them made to order at very little extra expense.

The clubs are waiting for you, all right. But there are many different combinations of shaft, swing weight and angle of clubface. Which is the right one for you?

It's a question you can't answer by yourself. You need help, and the best place to get it is from your pro. If you're going to be serious about the game, you're going to invest something like a couple of hundred dollars; why not invest another five dollars or ten dollars for self-protection? Take a lesson, or two lessons. Let the pro at your country club watch you hit a hundred balls or so. Let him analyze your swing and try you with different kinds of clubs. And then let him prescribe what kind of clubs will work best for you.

If you don't belong to a country club, have the pro at a public course or a good driving range help you. At the very least, buy your clubs at a shop where the salesman is a golfer himself and an expert on suiting the purchase to the purchaser. You wouldn't try to prescribe a pair of eyeglasses for yourself—and, to the golfer, clubs are as important as vision. The man who simply walks into a store, picks a set of clubs off the racks because he likes their looks, and buys them from a saleslady who doesn't know anything about them except the price and how to make out the sales slip, has only a remote chance of getting the clubs that will bring out his best game.

One thing for sure about clubs: you've got to be happy with them; you've got to feel comfortable; you've got to have confidence in them.

I'm something of a fanatic on the subject of clubs. I've always got at least a hundred of them in the basement workshop at my home, and on the tour I usually carry at least two full sets of woods, two more sets of irons and three or four putters. One bag of clubs is the one I'm relying on at the time. The others are part of my constant search for something better.

I wouldn't advise the average golfer to concern himself with such matters, but I myself take a great delight in fooling with my clubs and I think it helps me play a better game. If I try a new driver in practice and like it, except that it doesn't seem to have enough loft, I'll take it into the pro shop wherever I'm playing and grind the face into more of an angle. I'll pick up a new set of irons, try them for a while and then bend the heads to open or close them a little. I never go anywhere without a Swiss G.I. knife that I picked up at a hardware store in Kennedy Airport; it has everything from a razor-like blade that will cut the tape off a grip to a hacksaw that will cut through a steel shaft. I use it all the time to change grips or to take an eighth of an inch off the length of a shaft, or to unscrew the bottom plate of a wood so that I can add or subtract some weight.

I use a slightly heavier club, usually, in the winter. I feel stronger then and I like the feel of a little more weight. When the weather starts getting warmer, I go back to lighter clubs. As soon as it gets real hot, I unwind the grips and make them about a sixty-fourth of an inch smaller in diameter; I have the feeling that my fingers puff a little in the middle of summer and that I need a little less to hold on to. For a while I tried something new—for me, though an old idea with the manufacturers—concerning the grips. I unwound the tape on my drivers, put a thick string down the exact center of the back of the shaft and rewound the tape over the string. It seemed to provide a little better hold on the club, and a reference point for my grip.

Now I use grips that are built that way from the start, with a sort of V in the back to provide the reference point. These grips help me put the clubhead down behind the ball the same way every time. But I use them only on the driver, not on my irons. I don't want to put the irons down the same way every time; I may want to open the face or close it to vary my shots.

You probably know about my putter for it's had a lot of publicity. I've had it since 1957 and I've filed it, scraped it and soldered it until it looks nothing at all like the original. I can't even remember how it looked at the beginning. The only time I ever came close to throwing it away was after the first round of the 1962 British Open, when everything else about my game was going well but my putting was awful. My wife saved the day, both for the putter and for me. She noticed that I had finally managed to file so much off the bottom that all I had left was a blade so narrow that it kept hitting the ball below center. I immediately soldered some more metal to the bottom and my putting improved at once. Had it not been for Winnie's sharp eye, I probably would never have won the tournament.

I used to use a different putter, sometimes in every new round of a tournament; but in recent years I've always relied on Old Faithful and I think I'd be lost without her. But still I'm not satisfied; I'm constantly looking for a new putter that will give me even better results. A few times I've thought I'd found the new love for which I'm seeking, but when the chips were down in a tournament I always went back to Old Faithful.

This is probably just a personal idiosyncrasy, but I've never had a bag of clubs with which I've been completely satisfied. There's always been something a little bit wrong. They didn't all feel exactly alike or they didn't all swing exactly the same. This is in no way a reflection on the way golf clubs are made. When any reputable manufacturer tells you he's selling you a matched set of irons, believe me, he means it. You can put one of the clubs after another on the swing weight scale and the needle won't budge the breadth of a hair. But something happens to clubs as you use them. You can take two absolutely identical 5-irons, made at the same factory the same day, so perfectly alike that no engineer in the world could tell them apart. But if you use one of them for a while and then the other, all of a sudden they feel different. There seems to have been some subtle change in them. You still can't see any difference, but you could swing them blindfolded and tell which was which a hundred times out of a hundred. Maybe it isn't the clubs. Maybe something happens to me as I get better acquainted with a club.

I've often felt that if ever I could find the perfect set of clubs and the perfect putter, my troubles would be over. I'd hit my drives and my irons the same day after day, always long and straight, and I'd never have a three-putt green. I'm still looking for that set. But I'm also sure that this notion of mine is at least 50 per cent pipe dream; I keep pursuing it even though I know it is at least halfway foolish.

Common sense tells me that the equipment is the most standardized part of golf. The thing that makes a person blow hot and cold at the game, with a 65 one day and an 80 the next, is his own human frailty. Your brain isn't a calculating machine; you can't set it to perfect concentration and expect 100 per cent obedience. There are bound to be days when your thoughts get away from you, and something creeps in to spoil that concentration you need. Your body chemistry is different every day. Sometimes you feel great; sometimes you have a stomach ache. Sometimes you cut a finger, as I did on the trunk of my car just before the U.S. Open of 1962; after the doctors had taken three stitches in it I couldn't grip the club exactly as before no matter how hard I tried. Everybody in the world has bad days: the singer hits a clinker, the cashier makes the wrong change, the President muffs a question at his press conference. Why should the golfer be exempt?

What I personally hope to do, through constant practice and through the kind of concentration and mental discipline I have talked about, is cut down the margin of human error as much as I can. I hope to bring my mind and my body to the point where they can execute the golf swing almost automatically, day after day, regardless of what my body chemistry happens to be, almost regardless of whether I should be in bed nursing a cold or happen to have some stitches in a finger. You keep breathing no matter how you feel or what your mood happens to be, and maybe some day I can make the golf swing as natural and intimate a part of me as inhaling and exhaling.

Equipment plays a part in this, of course—and we come now to the moral for amateurs in what I have been saying.

How to Buy a Set of Clubs and the Right Ball for You

Once I've got a set of clubs put together, once I've filed a little bit here and there and changed the angle of the driver's clubface, once I've unwound and rewound the grips until they feel just right, I go with them. I know they're as right as I can get them an I know they aren't going to change overnight. They're a part of me and a part of what I have to reckon with on the golf course, like the size of my thumb.

Some days I pick up the driver and it feels nice and light. That's good. Some days I pick it up and it feels heavy. That's not so good. Almost every time I pick up the driver, first thing in the morning, it feels different somehow from the way it felt the day before. But I know that the club hasn't changed. *I've* changed. I'm just not feeling quite up to snuff or I'm not wide awake yet. So I stay with the club. I've got confidence in it. I know it's the best club there is for me. And, as I keep swinging it, gradually it begins to feel right again. The same with my putter. Some days I don't feel right with it and my first few putts are absurd. But it's my fault, not the club's—and sooner or later I start dropping them. That is, I start dropping them if I'm capable of it that day.

You've got to have the right kind of golf equipment, and that's why you need good advice before you buy it. You also need complete confidence in your equipment, and that's another reason for getting the advice. If you say "Eeeny, meeny, miney, mo" and reach for a set off the shelves, you're going to wonder every time you make a bad shot whether to blame yourself or the clubs. If you know you've got the right clubs, then you know whom to blame.

I experiment with my clubs between tournaments but, once the chips are down, I forget them. When I'm playing where it counts, I don't even want to think about my clubs. I want to take them for granted so that I can think about more important matters. I want to be free to devote all my attention to picking out the best spot on the fairway to aim at, or reading the slope and grain of the greens.

This should be your goal, too. Get the best clubs you can, as pre-scribed by the best expert available. Then forget them.

A few words about golf shoes. You've got to have them. You need those spikes to give you the solid footing on which everybody's golf game must be built. I'd never play without them—and I mean *never*. You can't swing while wearing spikeless shoes without slipping—or trying to prevent it. You're bound to fall into some bad habits.

About golf balls. Like the shafts of the clubs, they're made in various types to suit various kinds of hitters. We pros use the highest compression ball that is legal under P.G.A. rules. It gives us the greatest possible distance. But to use this kind of ball to advantage you have to hit it a real lick; if you have ever seen a photograph of the ball at the moment of impact, when a strong-armed pro like Jack Nicklaus hits it, you'll have noticed that the ball is almost completely flat where the club has struck; it looks as if it had been cut in two. It takes that kind of pressure to make the high-compression ball take off.

The ordinary golfer actually gets more distance out of a ball with lower compression. This kind is designed to produce the maximum distance for the average swinger, and it does. Moreover, it has a little heavier cover and won't cut so easily. You'll get more distance on each shot and also more use out of each ball.

I have quite a few friends who are just average golfers, but insist on using the highest-compression ball they can buy. I suppose it's a matter of pride with them. But, believe me, pride is a bad thing to have on a golf course—and in this case it's costing them money as well as strokes. I'd like to sell you lots of Palmer golf balls, of course, but no more than you really need.

CHAPTER XI

THE MENTAL APPROACH TO THE FIRST THREE HOLES

WHEN I WAS A YOUNG PRO, I had the feeling that nobody on the tour concentrated very much in the early stages of a tournament. It was a natural suspicion for it is very difficult in any sport to take the beginning as seriously as the end. You see more errors in the early innings of a baseball game than in the late ones. There have been a number of great pitchers who were almost invincible if they got past the first inning, but were sometimes knocked out before they settled down to work. You see a lot of sloppy play in the first few minutes of football and basketball games. If it happens elsewhere, why not in a golf tournament, where you have sixty-nine more holes to make up for anything you do wrong on the first three?

But I was wrong. Dead wrong. I have learned since that everybody in professional golf works as hard on the first tee as any other. The few players about whom I was right—those who were taking it easy at the start—have long since dropped out of the tour. They couldn't make the grade.

It's the old story of what I said earlier: If you don't birdie the first hole, you can't birdie them all. The first three holes of a golf match count just as much as the last three. As a matter of fact, they are probably even more important, because of their tremendous psychological effect.

Oh, it's great to overcome a bad start and come from behind, but it isn't easy. A bad start can discourage you, throwing your game off completely. We pros sometimes find that we have shot ourselves right out of a tournament on the first nine. The average player, if he starts off badly, finds it almost impossible to pull his game together. His confidence and concentration are gone for the day; he may as well go home.

How much better it is to start off hot as a firecracker and not have to come from behind. For one thing, it's physically easier to score well on the early holes when you are fresh and strong than on the late holes when you are tired. For another, a good start sets you up mentally and gives you the confidence you need to keep playing your best.

I know that I myself play my best when I start well. You won't read about it so often in the newspapers, because it's not as dramatic as a come-from-behind finish, but it's true. In the Masters of 1964, for example, I was tied for the lead after the first round and in front all the rest of the way. I always felt in charge, I felt great, there was never any doubt in my mind that I was going to win. Then there was the Phoenix Open of 1962, which I began with birdies on the first six holes. I won that tournament by twelve strokes, the biggest margin I've ever had. That's what a good start can do for you!

You have to keep reminding yourself all the time that the first three holes count, for it's easy to forget. Even in an eighteen-hole round, the whole day seems to loom ahead of you. If you lose the first hole, there's always the second. And if you lose the second hole, too, there are still sixteen to go. . . . But if you fall into this lackadaisical mental trap, your day can be ruined before you know it. You're hopelessly beaten in your match; you haven't got a chance of breaking 100 or 90 or 75 or whatever was your goal for the day, and the rest of the round is just a chore and a nuisance. Chalk up another golf round spoiled by carelessness in the early stages.

Most golfers have a physical as well as a mental problem on the first three holes. Yes, I'm about to bring up that old bromide about warming up before playing. I know you've heard it a hundred times. I know that you are sick of hearing someone say, pompously and as if it were a brand new discovery, "Have you ever thought about the fact that golf is the only game in the world where the players don't warm up? They warm up in baseball, football, tennis, everything else —but we golfers step right up to the first tee and drive off."

All right, it's a bromide and a bore. But it's true. If you have been playing without warming up, I will absolutely guarantee that you can cut three strokes a round off your score—without changing anything else about your game—if you will just take a few minutes to get ready.

I personally would never think of playing without spending at least a half hour on the practice green and the practice tee. I like to try some short putts and some long ones, some chips, some irons and quite a few drives. This prepares me both physically and mentally for my round. My muscles get loosened up, my hands get the feel of the clubs. And psychologically I put aside whatever other thoughts have been on my mind and begin to concentrate on the golf ball. I get relaxed. I get confident.

Even the pros who seldom practice at any other time practice before they play. Some of them get out to the course a full hour ahead of their starting time. They may hit as many as fifty shots off the practice tee, and try fifty putts. When they step up to the first tee, they know they are ready.

Why don't you try it? If you can devote four hours of your day to playing your round, surely you can take a few more minutes to prepare yourself and make certain you will do your best—and also get the maximum fun out of the game. It's no pleasure at all to walk up to that first tee feeling stiff and unsure of yourself and muff your drive right in front of all the people standing around there—as so many golfers do.

Even fifteen minutes on the practice tee will help immeasurably. Check your grip. Think for a moment about the fundamentals. Then hit a few 8-iron shots, some 5-irons, some long irons and some drives. Don't think about too many different things at once, just the few simple rules of the golf shot. Don't get so engrossed in analyzing your swing as to risk confusion. All you have to do is get squared away. Even if you don't change a thing while you're warming up, you will still play better. You'll be loose and limber. You'll be *ready*.

What if you don't have a practice tee? Well, that's a handicap, and I know it's a handicap that golfers have to face at many public courses and even quite a few private clubs. But it isn't fatal. Hit some chips to the practice green; even chip shots will loosen your muscles and sharpen your concentration. And swing some of your longer clubs. It's better if you can actually hit the ball and watch the results, but it's not absolutely essential. Just swinging the club for ten or fifteen minutes will help a lot. You haven't been using those golfing muscles while you sat at a desk all week; they need time to get back into action. They've got to get warmed up and lubricated before they can function.

But a word of warning. No matter how much time you spend warming up, there's nothing that says you can't have a bad first hole anyway. You can have a bad hole at any time on the golf course. Even when you are playing one of the best rounds of your life, you may suddenly go wrong on the sixth hole, or the twelfth or the eighteenth —or, for that matter, the first.

One year I stepped up to the first tee in the Eastern Open at Baltimore feeling just great. I had been playing well for weeks. I had felt good on the practice tee. My practice shots had been long and straight. The weather was nice and warm and I had worked up a good sweat. My muscles felt loose, eager. Mentally, I had exactly the combination of concentration and relaxation I always strive for. I was sure I was going to have a good round. I was sure of it in my conscious mind and in my unconscious mind and in my bones.

I took an easy, confident swing with my driver and the ball hooked out of bounds. I had wasted two strokes before the tournament had even begun. In disgust, I turned to Doug Ford, who was next up to hit, and said, "Hell, I think I'll put the ball in my pocket and go home."

Doug said quietly, "The way you've been playing, you can afford to spot the field two strokes. Go ahead and hit another."

It was all I needed to jolt me back to reality. I had been foolish to be discouraged: anybody can hit a ball out of bounds at any moment. The thing to do was forget it, put it out of my mind entirely and start all over. I teed up another ball and hit it far and straight. With this ball I had a birdie, giving me a bogey for the first hole counting the penalty strokes. I was two strokes under par after the first five holes and went on to win the tournament.

So there are two morals in this chapter, and if they seem a little contradictory, they're not. The first is to play your best from the very outset—the first holes count as much as any others. The second is not to let a bad tee shot or a bad score on the first hole throw you if it takes place. Chalk it up as just one of those things. If you're warmed up physically and mentally and if you're concentrating, your touch will come back.

CHAPTER XII

THE MENTAL APPROACH
TO THE LAST
THREE HOLES

ONE GOLF HOLE I'll never forget is the eighteenth at Augusta, in the Masters of 1961. It was the last day of the tournament. Everything about my game had pulled together and I had come from four strokes behind. All I needed, as I stood on the eighteenth tee, was a par 4 to win, a bogey 5 to tie.

I hit one of my best drives of the day, right in the center of the fairway, about 260 yards out, not more than 150 yards from the green. I walked down the fairway feeling great. My friends in the crowd came up to slap me on the back. I was in, I couldn't miss. I had broken all golfing precedent by winning the Masters for the second year in a row. My mind was grinning all over.

If you remember your golfing history, you know what happened next. I took a 7-iron to the green, came off the ball a little, sent the shot out on the low side and faded it, right into a sand trap. When I walked up to the trap I saw that the ball lay almost against the rear bank. I had my choice. I could play it safe out of the trap, not aiming for the hole at all, and settle for a 5 and a tie. Or I could gamble and go for the hole and victory.

I gambled, and hit the shot too clean. The ball sailed high over the green and into the rough on the far side, an impossible position. I had all I could do to get down in three more strokes—for a double-bogey 6 and a tie not for first place but for second. (See the photographs of this disaster on pages 106–107.)

I had blown it. I had held victory in my hands and had let it slip through. It taught me a lesson, I can tell you that. I brooded about it all that winter and now I have a philosophy about the final holes of a tournament—or of a single round of golf—that I think will keep me from ever making such a mistake again.

If I ever find myself in a similar situation, with a great drive off the final tee and everybody crowding around to congratulate me, you'll never again see me grinning like a fool at the compliments. I won't let anybody slap my back. I'll say, "Well, now, let's just wait a minute here and see what happens. Nobody wins a tournament until the ball is in the hole and the scorecards are signed."

If you lose your concentration on the golf course, you're done for—and, as I found out the hard way, you can lose it fastest of all through overconfidence. You've got to have your mind on the ball. You can't let it go to counting unhatched chickens. While you're counting, the chickens are all going to disappear.

But suppose this: suppose that history could repeat itself and for all my sustained concentration I should miss my second shot again and wind up in that same spot at the back of the sand trap. What would I do then? Would I gamble—or would I play it safe?

I'd gamble. I'd be a lot more careful with the shot; I'd concentrate with every ounce of determination I could muster, but I'd still go for the flag. Let me tell you why, because it is something that comes up all the time in golf and is something that applies particularly to amateurs.

I have a friend who took up golf late in life and is never going to be a champion, but who can hit the ball pretty well when he puts his mind to it. He took quite a few lessons; he knows how to grip the club and how to swing it and you'd think he'd be a good, steady 85-to-90 shooter. Yet he's never in his life broken 100. He's had a lot of chances. He has frequently come up to the final holes of a round needing nothing better than three 6s to come in with a 99. Once all he needed was two 6s and a 7. He had nineteen strokes left for three holes—and he blew it.

I know why. He gets to thinking about how much margin he has. He says to himself, "Even if I miss my tee shot on the sixteenth, I've

BAD DAY AT AUGUSTA

With the Masters all but won, I blast out and over the eighteenth green into the rough on the far side. But worse is to come . . .

1

. . . back on the green after my chip, still with a good chance to tie, I blow the putt and the tournament with it.

still got it made." He's thinking so hard about what will happen if he misses the tee shot that he actually does miss it. That's part of the psychology of the game, as I've been trying to show. You have to play every shot to the hilt, as if your life depended on it. If you start figuring that a shot isn't important, if you decide you don't have to make it, then you're almost bound to muff it.

Well, he misses the tee shot, and then starts making some more advance excuses. He tells himself that he doesn't have to try extra hard to hit the green with his second. He decides he's too far out anyway. He'll just bang the ball somewhere up in the general direction of the hole. Then he'll pitch on with his third shot and still have three putts for his 6. He bangs the ball all right, much too carelessly, and finds to his chagrin that instead of an easy little pitch he's still got a full 7-iron or 6-iron to go.

The story is too gruesome to finish, but you can imagine the rest of it. On that day when all he needed was a 19 on the final three holes, he took a 24!

The same thing, on a less spectacular scale, frequently happens to the good amateur, the man who consistently shoots in the high 70s or low 80s. His ambition is to shoot even par some day. And some day it happens—almost. He comes up to the final three holes a stroke under par. All he needs is two pars and a bogey.

On all the previous holes he's been doing his almighty best. He's been trying for birdies every time. On the short holes, he hasn't been content just to aim the ball anywhere on the green; he's been going straight for the flag to leave himself the shortest possible putt for a bird. On the par 4s he's been trying to get good and far out with his drive, and then hit his second shot stiff to the pin. Now, all of a sudden, he goes conservative. You could be even harsher and say he "goes chicken." All he wants is those two pars and a bogey. He stops trying to play his best and settles for his second best.

Nearly every time he blows it. The minute he stops going for the birds, the minute he decides to be content with a par, something happens to his concentration. He's thinking that he can get away with being a little sloppy and the message seeps down into his reflexes. Up to this point in the round, he's been on top of his game; he's managed to maintain that ideal mixture of concentration and relaxation. Now he lets it get away from him. The decision to settle for two pars and a bogey is an almost automatic guarantee that he will take something nearer two bogeys and a double bogey. His opportunity for a par round goes out the window. Afterward he hates himself for days.

To play golf well, you have to play aggressively and when the temptation comes to let down, as it can so easily do when you reach those crucial last three holes of a good round, you have to resist it with all the will power at your command. I don't mean by this that you have to make any foolish gambles. When your ball is sitting nicely on the eighteenth green and you still have two strokes left to get the score that has been your lifetime ambition or to win a match from an opponent you love to beat, it would be silly to charge your first putt and run the risk of going so far past the hole that you can't get back. In a situation like that, I'd settle for two putts every time, and so would every other pro. I'd *hope* to hole out with my first putt, but I'd never go for all or nothing; I'd never stroke the ball so that it would either drop in or go 10 feet past. It's only common sense, under these circumstances, to be a little conservative.

But in general, let me say again, you have to play aggressively if you want to play your best. This is true in every sport. (How many times have you seen a college basketball team, with a 10-point lead going into the last few minutes of a game, decide to hang on, play strictly defensively—and get nosed out? And have you noticed how the professional football teams, who have learned through long experience the dangers of trying to play safe, keep throwing those passes even when they're 14 points ahead?)

It is especially true in this game of mind over matter called golf. The only time in recent years I ever forgot to play aggressively it cost me a tournament. This was in the Wilmington Open of 1958, a week before the Masters. I finished in a tie with Howie Johnson and we had a Monday playoff. I figured I could handle Howie pretty easily the way I had been playing and my mind was mostly on the Masters. So I didn't try to win big. I decided to settle for a nice easy win without extending myself. I was just out for a pleasant, relaxing round of golf to help keep me in shape for the Masters. So what happened? Howie Johnson had a bad round and came in with a

77—but he beat me because I had an even worse round. The truth of the matter was that I beat myself by thinking small. It cured me forever.

There is another hazard during the final holes of a golf round, not so much for us professionals as for the amateur, and especially for the amateur who doesn't play often. To a man who has been sitting at a desk all week, who hasn't walked any farther than from his front door to the bus stop and back again in the evening, a round of golf can be pretty tiring. Many weekend players come up to those last three holes feeling a little beat. Their legs are tired; their hands are starting to hurt; their shoulders are getting stiff.

The tendency, when you feel like this, is to try too hard. You know you're tired, you're not as strong as you were on the first nine; so you feel you have to put an extra effort into hitting the ball. You think you have to wind up a little more, take a longer backswing, press for some kind of hidden reserve of physical strength that will make up for your fatigue. But when you're tired, your legs can't move as fast as usual. You can't get the same kind of body action. Trying too hard can only result in overswinging and getting off-balance, so now you miss your shots. Your game goes all to pieces, and what started out as a good round winds up a fiasco.

The secret of living with fatigue on the golf course is not to try harder, but to settle for hitting the ball with a little less than your maximum strength. This is the time to take a shorter backswing, not à longer one. The swing has to become *more* compact, not *less* compact. You have to play now as if you were ten years older, because fatigue has actually made your muscles ten years older for the time being. Your drives can't possibly be as long as they were earlier in the day. You're going to have to use a 5-iron, maybe even a 4-, where on the first nine you were using a 6-. The pros do this all the time when they feel tired. I've done it hundreds of times. You should try it too.

Does this contradict what I said earlier about playing aggressively? No, not at all. You're still going to think positively. You're going to keep thinking in terms of birdies or of pars or whatever is a reasonable goal for your kind of golfer. You're going to stay determined to do the best you possibly can—*under the circumstances.*

But the circumstances have changed. The muscles that were so eager on the front nine have now been replaced by muscles that would just as soon be under a hot shower. And you have to take this into account. Not to take it into account would be foolhardy. Your body knows you're tired. The unconscious and subconscious parts of your brain know it. If you refuse to admit with the conscious part of your mind that you're tired, if you command your muscles to hit those drives just as far as before, then only one thing can happen. In trying to carry out the command, your nerves and muscles and reflexes are going to stretch and strain. Your swing is going to get away from you and you're going to lose that firm sense of easy balance that you need. Your game is going to collapse completely.

If you've been the kind of player who often takes a 42 on the first nine and a 53 on the back nine, this is probably what has been happening. Next time you come up to the final holes, take stock. How do your legs feel? Your shoulders? Honestly, now? Are they getting tired? It is nothing to be ashamed of. Confess it and alter your game accordingly. Settle for a shorter swing. Maybe your opponent is feeling the pace just as much as you, but isn't as smart as you. The sixteenth, seventeenth and eighteenth don't have to spoil your day—you can even win there!

CHAPTER XIII

HOW TO TALK YOURSELF INTO BETTER PUTTING

THE AVERAGE GOLFER, even if he spends a good deal of time on the practice tee with his driver, seldom practices putting. The touring pros are just the opposite. Even the pros who hate to spend time on the practice tee keep working all the time with their putters. If they're staying at a hotel that has a putting green, you'll see them out there by the hour. If you visit their rooms at night, you'll probably find them hitting balls across the carpet.

The average golfer has a tendency to be lackadaisical about his 2-foot and 3-foot putts; he walks up to them quickly, thinking about something else, and misses far more of them than he should. He walks away shrugging his shoulders, as if it were fate—and on the next tee he grits his teeth and half kills himself working on his drive. The pro concentrates as hard on the 2-footers as on anything else in golf. When he misses one, he wants to know why. What went wrong? Did he push? Did he pull? Did he move his body? Did he jerk his hands? You'll see him standing there thinking, taking one practice stroke after another with the putter, trying to correct himself. He concentrates as hard on his putts and spends as much labor over them as on his drives.

A little arithmetic will show you why. On a standard par 72 golf course, thirty-six strokes are allowed to get the ball from tee to green, and the other thirty-six strokes are for putts. Putting is half the game. That little 2-foot shot you make with the putter counts just as much as that 250-yard shot you are hoping to make on your drive.

The pro knows that there are only three ways he can make a birdie. He can birdie the par 5s by hitting the ball so far, off the tee and then off the fairway, that he reaches the green in two strokes instead of the three that par allows him. He can birdie any hole by laying his approach shot—or his tee shot on the par threes—so close to the pin that the putt is a mere formality. Or he can learn to sink middle-distance and long-distance putts and take one stroke on the green instead of the regulation two.

Of these three possibilities, the third is by far the most productive. After all, there are only four par 5 holes on most courses. No golfer ever yet born has been so accurate with his irons that he can send every approach shot over an unerring course of from 100 to 200 yards and stop it within 5 feet of the pin every time. But in each round of golf there are eighteen glorious opportunities to drop the ball into the hole with your first putt.

To the average player who wants to improve his score, putting is even more important, if anything, than it is to the pro. The average player can't reach a par-5 green in fewer than three strokes. He's going to miss the green entirely with many of his approach shots and his tee shots on the par 3s. If he wants to shoot par or anything close to it, he's got to sink those first putts. And if instead of sinking his first putt he goes to the other unhappy extreme of missing some of his second putts, so that he winds up with a lot of three-putt greens, his score will go right up into orbit.

Keep a record of what happens on the greens in your next few rounds. Even for the best of putters, of course, the number of strokes on the green will vary considerably from round to round; it depends on how close you are getting to the pin with your approach shots and chips. But in general you can use the par figures as a guide. If you are average thirty-six putts a round, you are missing the best of all opportunities for improving your score. If you find you are averaging more than thirty-six, you have put your finger on one of the most damaging faults in your game.

It's the one that can be most easily corrected for, of all the aspects of golf, putting is the most obviously and undeniably improvable by concentration and practice. Not everybody has the physical equipment to knock the ball 250 yards off the tee. Not everybody has the coordination required for precise accuracy with the approach irons.

But almost everybody can learn to be a good putter. Even the most fragile of the women pros putt as well as the two hundred-pound male pros. You see eight-year-old boys and girls who can putt as if the ball were magnetized, also seventy- and eighty-year-old men.

The mechanical side of putting is hardly worth mentioning. You can hold the putter any way you like. I personally use the reverse overlapping grip, as you can see in the drawing, with all the fingers of my right hand on the club and the index finger of the left hand lying on top of them, pointed straight down the shaft. This is the most generally used of all putting grips. But some golfers get good results with a double overlap (like my grip except that the little finger of the right hand is locked between the index and second finger of the left hand) or with the same interlocking or baseball grip discussed in Chapter 2. It's all a matter of personal preference.

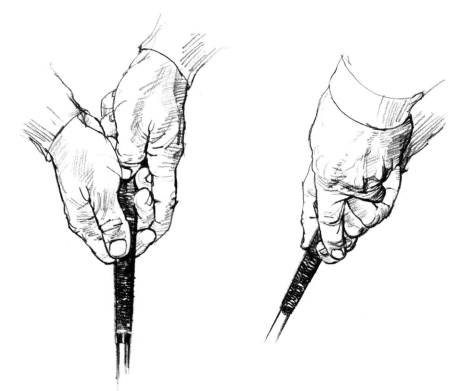

Most of the touring pros today use the same putting grip as I do, shown here in a front and side view.

How to Talk Yourself into Better Putting

As long as your hands are comfortable and you have the feeling that your right hand is ready to stroke the ball with precision, you're in business.

You can use any kind of stance you want. Most golfers putt from a square stance, with the feet set evenly on the line they want the ball to take. This is the way I stand myself. But Jack Nicklaus gets good results from an extremely closed stance, with his right foot drawn well back from the line. Other golfers like to open the stance a little. Some golfers stand erect and some like to crouch. My own most noticeable characteristic, I guess, is that I stand knock-kneed. I do it because I feel that it locks my body in position. Again, it doesn't matter what stance you use—as long as it works.

Some people, myself included, are wrist putters; we move the club by breaking our wrists while holding our arms nearly motionless. Others are arm putters; they keep their wrists stiff and stroke the ball by moving their arms. There's nothing that says wrist putting is more accurate than arm putting, or vice versa. It's up to the individual.

Many golfers swear by a mallet-type putter, many others by the blade type. My own Old Faithful, as I have mentioned, is a blade. But, again, there's nothing that says one is actually better than the other and the next putter I go to, if I ever change, may very well be a mallet. Some golfers own several different kinds of putters; they have one they like to use on fast greens, another for slow greens and so on. There seems to be a general feeling that the mallet type is better on slow greens, perhaps because it looks heavier and more substantial, as if it would hit the ball harder with less effort. Personally, I feel just the opposite. If I were the kind of golfer who switched putters depending on the course, I would use a mallet for fast greens and a blade for slow greens. But don't ask me why, for again it's all in the feel. And I don't think I'll ever be inclined to carry putters for courses anyway. My own theory is that you should find the one you like and then stick with it under all circumstances, on the theory that the more familiar you are with your club the better the results.

About the only time it pays to switch putters, I think, is when your touch has gone off and you can't get the ball in the hole no matter how hard you try. When that happens, it often helps to change to a different putter for a round or two, then go back to your favorite.

"Old Faithful," my much-worked-on putter

You're in a rut with the old putter; you've lost confidence; you're afraid you'll never get your touch back. The new putter makes you feel better, and after a little while you can return to the one you really like and use it with confidence again. Why it should work that way I don't exactly know. Perhaps the different feel of the new putter shakes you out of some bad physical or mental habits you've acquired. Or perhaps the whole thing is superstition, like the lift you get from finding a four-leaf clover. At any rate I myself switched putters a couple of times in '64, and found this helpful in getting better results with Old Faithful.

Some very good putters believe they do better hitting uphill than downhill; if they are close enough to the green to think about such fine points, they will chip the ball to stop below the hole, if anything, rather than above it. Others believe they do better downhill. I think these beliefs are more fancied than real. I personally prefer an uphill putt to a downhill putt, but only because there is less danger of going way past the hole if I miss. My observations over the years tell me that I sink just as many downhill putts as uphill putts; there's no real difference at all.

How to Talk Yourself into Better Putting

There is only one mechanical secret to putting, in my confirmed opinion, and this is holding still. Your body has to be totally motionless while you stroke the ball—and so, as in all golf shots, does your head. (You can see how motionless I stand in the multiple-exposure photograph below.) If you sway, you're bound to miss. This is why I stand knock-kneed. Having my knees close together gives me the feeling that I'm so solid above the ball that I couldn't move if I tried. I could, of course—anybody can, no matter how he stands. It's a constant temptation and you have to watch it all the time.

The way to learn to keep your body and head still, and to stroke the ball along a straight line, is to practice. You can do it on a putting green or even a carpet; many a player has suddenly blossomed out in the springtime as a great putter because he spent a few minutes a day over the winter months stroking the ball over the livingroom rug.

But you have to practice putting as seriously as any other golf shot, with your mind as well as your body. It does no good at all simply to bang the ball toward the hole, cheer when it drops and feel depressed when it misses. You have to stroke and analyze, stroke and analyze. It dropped that time: what did you do right? It missed that time: what did you do wrong? Did your head move? Your body? Was your stroke jerky? Are you constantly pushing the ball off to the right, or pulling it to the left? Were you thinking about something else while you should have been concentrating on the shot?

If you putt without analyzing and the only mental reaction you have during practice is to feel good on days when your average is high and bad on days when it is low, you're not learning anything. You're simply getting more confirmed in whatever bad habits you already have. For the kind of practice that improves your putting, you have to think before and after every shot, just as when you are practicing with the driver.

You need practice too in reading the greens. You have to know how much break to expect as a result of a slope in the green, and how much to expect from the grain of the grass. You have to learn how much harder to putt against the grain than with the grain. These are things you learn through observation. Too many amateurs sink their putt or miss it and walk away without giving a moment's thought to what happened and why. They seem to feel that putting is mostly a matter of instinct and luck. Well, I'll grant that there's *some* luck to it, especially on greens that are not well kept. But mostly it's a science. Except for the occasional rough spot or totally hidden dip in a green, the ball will go exactly where your club makes it go, plus the slope and grain of the green—and these last two factors will affect the ball the same way time after time. *They are predictable.*

You've heard, of course, of missing putts on the "amateur side" or on the "pro side"—phrases which grew out of the fact that most amateurs tend to underestimate the effect of a slope in the green, when they have a sidehill lie, and let the ball dribble ignominiously below the hole, whereas the pros always take full account of the slope and tend to err on the high side, if at all. But this is not the worst putting sin of the average golfer. There are thousands of players— watch for them and you will see what I mean—who are consistently short on every uphill putt and consistently long on every downhill putt. And I mean *every*. They do it time after time, like a robin who keeps pecking at automobile hubcaps, refusing to admit that his re- flection is not an enemy robin.

It can only mean that they aren't paying attention. They're not analyzing their putts. They haven't concentrated on the putting game even the little bit that it takes to learn that a ball has to be hit harder to travel uphill than downhill. No wonder they are totally baffled by sidehill lies and by greens with a lot of grain.

Most golf books contain instructions for reading a green, and I could offer you some rules of thumb, too—but I won't. I feel that every golfer should learn his own method. Reading the green, judg- ing whether it's slow or fast and calculating which way the ball will break and how far are matters that each individual should work out for himself, like his putting grip and his putting stance. The only way I can help you is to get you started thinking about these things, not by giving you a little set of rules that would only serve as another excuse for never stopping to think at all.

Now about that mental attitude known as confidence. It means everything, of course. If you have played golf at all, you know that when you walk up to a putt expecting to miss it, you do. You know that on days when you've putted well on the early holes and have the happy feeling that everything is going to drop for you, you sink a surprising number of putts from distances that amaze you.

If you think you're a good putter, if you keep telling yourself how great you are, it certainly helps. I've often played with a man more or less new to the game who kept telling me that he wasn't any good as yet with the woods and the irons, but by golly he did know how to putt. He figured he could putt as well as anybody, the pros included. At the time what he said was laughable, because in all truth his putting was atrocious. He moved his head, moved his body, had no idea how to read a green and sprayed his putts in every direction, missing low, high, short and long. But a year later I would play with the same fellow again, and darned if he wasn't a good putter by then. He believed in himself and his belief came true.

We pros do something that I think is very bad psychology. Because putting is such an important part of scoring, we brood about it too much and do too much complaining. Ask almost any pro any evening of the week what kind of a round he had that day and he'll say "Man, I was hitting the ball great. I was on every green. If I could only have dropped my putts, I'd have torn the course apart. But I want to tell you, I'm the world's worst putter, bar none." I've said it often myself. I probably said it last night and I'll probably say it tomorrow.

Mostly it's just talk. We aren't as serious as we sound. We don't really have an inferiority complex about putting or we'd never last as pros. When we grouse about putting we're just letting off steam, so it probably doesn't hurt us. On the other hand, it certainly doesn't help us. It would be far better if we did just the opposite and bragged about our putting even when it was at its worst.

If you have a friend with whom you play frequently, and whom you'd like to help play better golf—or am I daydreaming about a kind of friendship that doesn't exist on a golf course? —you might try an experiment. Without telling him, figure out about how many putts a round he takes. Then start complimenting his putting at every opportunity. Tell him what a great touch he's got. Praise him for every putt he drops and sympathize with him for every one he misses. Tell him the ball hit a rough spot or a hidden dip. Ask him how he holds his putter and how he manages to keep his head so still. At the end of a couple of months, calculate how many putts he's averaging now and see if you haven't knocked three or four strokes off the total. That's a lot of strokes. If you don't believe it, try to figure some time how far you would have to lengthen your driving average to save three or four shots a round.

You can do the same thing in reverse to a rival you'd like to beat more often, but I don't advise it. Golf is too fine a game for that sort of thing. What I do advise, and most strongly, is that you use the psychology on yourself. It's an absolute fact that you are bound to improve your putting if you study it and practice it as I have suggested. So get to work with zest and confidence. There's no limit to how good you can be. Improvement should come fast. You're going to be the world's greatest putter. In fact you're well on your way to that goal right now. Be confident, my friend, and watch them start dropping.

CHAPTER XIV

THE SECRET OF
ACCURATE DRIVING

EVERY GOLFER DREAMS of being long and straight off the tee. There's nothing more spectacular and soul-satisfying in golf than a drive that takes off like a jet, bores a straight line up and up toward the clouds, then finally drops in a long and graceful arc, finding its way unerringly over a 275-yard path to the exact spot where you aimed it.

A long drive is good for the ego. It sets you up and puts you in a frame of mind to play the rest of your shots well.

It's a great competitive asset, especially in match play. It keeps your opponents worried; they have to scramble to catch up with you. And you have the advantage of watching their second shots before you have to make up your mind about your own next move.

Yes, there's nothing like it—if you can manage it. Unfortunately, not every golfer can. I don't for one moment take back what I said earlier about my strong opinion, derived from my father and verified by my own experience, that you don't have to have a great deal of natural ability to learn to score pretty well at golf. But the drive, I think, is the exception. You do have to have a lot of natural ability to hit the ball 275 yards. This is something that takes a certain combination of reflexes, strength, coordination and above-average timing.

You can see what I mean if you compare the men pros and the women pros. The women are great; their scores are fabulous. Yet

even the best of the women pros average about 35 yards less off the tee than the men.

I want to preface my remarks about the driver, therefore, with this thought: If you never in your life manage to hit the ball 275 yards, or 250 yards, or even 200 yards, you can still be a good golfer. I wouldn't want you to strive too hard for distance off the tee. I certainly wouldn't want you to be discouraged if you fail to attain it. All you can do is work on your drive until you have made it as good as you can within your physical limitations. At this point you should concentrate on other aspects of the game. In my own case, I know that 275 yards, on the average, is the best I can do. If I spent all of my time trying to stretch it to 285 yards, I would only hurt my game. I keep practicing with the driver, of course; I have to practice in order to maintain that 275-yard average. But I'm not trying for additional distance now, nor concentrating on the driver to the detriment of my other clubs.

For the amateur, as a matter of fact, the long drive can be a dubious asset. The chances are that he can't play or practice enough to keep any part of his game absolutely sharp. His drives can't possibly all be down the middle. (Even the pros who play every day don't achieve that kind of perfection with the driver.) And the farther his drives go, the more chance they have of getting into trouble. I know dozens of power-hitting amateurs who play a tremendous game on their good days—but on most days are never out of the woods. They win big when they're hitting the ball straight, but they lose more matches than they win.

I finally managed to master the driver—if I or any other golfer can ever be said to have mastered anything at all about this tricky and elusive game—when I was thirty years old. By that time I had probably played at least three thousand rounds of golf, far more than the average person plays in a lifetime. I had been swinging the club for twenty-six years and had spent goodness knows how many thousands of hours on the course and on the practice tee before I felt that I could really count on my drives to go as far and as straight as I wanted. Even now I can't count on them every time, just most of the time. It all goes to show what a frustrating club the driver can be.

Like almost every other player who has eventually become a pro, I

124

started with a hook. All my tee shots had a spin that made them travel from right to left. Too often for comfort, they got away from me. I was what is called a duck-hooker. I knew through sad experience that at least once a round, sometimes on tee after tee, my drive would take off very low, duck sharply to the left and wind up in the deep rough or out of bounds. It was a discouraging piece of knowledge to carry around.

I was a duck-hooker all through childhood, through high school and in my early years on the golf team at Wake Forest College. I was winning lots of matches and some amateur tournaments, but I could never be confident on the tee. I never knew when to expect the trouble.

All the while I was going to Wake Forest my best friend was Bud Worsham, a fine gentleman and a great golfer who might be dominating the game today had he not been killed in an automobile accident in our senior year. He was the brother of Lew Worsham, who won the world professional championship in 1953 and the National Open in 1947, and is now the pro at Oakmont Country Club in Pittsburgh. Well, one night in 1949, during the North and South Amateur, Bud and I were playing gin rummy with a third brother, Herman Worsham, and Herman brought up the matter of my hook. He said that Lew had been watching me and had expressed the opinion that I was holding the driver with too exaggerated a version of the strong grip that I discussed in Chapter 2.

He didn't put it in exactly these words because this was long before people had begun talking about the "strong" versus the "weak" grip. But even in 1949, Lew Worsham had come to the conclusion that the position of the hands would affect the action of the ball, even though he had not worked out all the theoretical details or reasons. If I moved my left hand more to the left, he had suggested to Herman, I might get rid of that duck hook.

Next day on the practice tee I hit a drive in my usual way and saw that Herman was right about how I was holding the club. As I looked down, I could see three knuckles of the left hand—a lot of knuckles. I moved my hands to the left until the Vs were pointing straight up and down and hit some shots. The results were wonderful. I got just as much distance as ever and the ball traveled much straighter. I tried shot after shot and never once did I duck hook. I went to bed that night with sore hands, but elated.

On the following day I played Frank Stranahan in the semifinal round of the tournament. I teed off with complete confidence and after three holes I was 2 up. I can hardly tell you how good I felt. I had discovered the secret of the drive. I had the game licked. I began wondering what my score would be: a 68? a 66? maybe even a 64?

We stopped for lunch and resumed our match. Suddenly everything went to pieces. Stranahan beat me 12 up and 11 to go—the worst defeat I ever took in my life. On the last nine he felt so sorry for me that he was giving me lessons, showing me how to grip and swing the club—and I was so completely despondent that I was trying my best to follow his advice, even where it meant changing the habits of many years' standing. It was one of the worst days, all in all, of my life.

Afterward, I had to do some soul-searching. There were two problems haunting me. The first concerned what Lew Worsham had suggested: Should I stick with his advice about the position of the hands or go back to my old method? The second concerned some of the things Frank Stranahan had told me: Was my game really as unsound as he had seemed to think and, if so, should I give up golf or try to start over?

I solved the second problem first. Up to this time I had never listened to advice from anybody but my father, and I decided that I never would again. I was convinced that my game was sound. Aside from any question of the position of the hands, my grip was basically all right. I couldn't see how any change would be for the better. I was learning to keep my head steady and that was the main foundation for the swing. As for the swing itself, perhaps I could learn a little better rhythm and timing, but basically what my father had taught me was the right and natural way to do it.

In my match with Frank Stranahan, everything had gone wrong. I had lost my confidence and my concentration. I was tense instead of relaxed. I tried too hard, and the harder I tried the worse I got. I was all off-balance; my muscles were tied in knots. But in trying to help me, I concluded, Stranahan had only made matters worse. From now on, I resolved, I would never again lose faith in my own game and let someone else try to change it. I believed in my game and henceforth I would always go along with it.

But what about the position of the hands? I experimented, swinging the club and trying to discover how the position of my hands on the shaft affected the action of the clubhead down in the hitting area. It seemed to me that Lew Worsham was right. The way I held the driver in the past, the natural action of my arms and wrists, down in that crucial area of a few inches where the clubhead comes into the ball and sends it on its way, was bound to close the face of the club and produce a hook. Sometimes the action of the clubface was bound to be exaggerated and the result would be a duck hook. If I moved my left hand over and kept the V straight up and down, my natural wrist and arm action would bring the clubhead into the ball square. I was almost sure to get more accuracy.

I made my decision and I stuck with it, although it wasn't easy. That entire summer was a nightmare. I couldn't do anything right. I lost to players whom I had always beaten easily in the past. My average score was somewhere up in the 80s.

The temptation to go back to my old grip was almost overwhelming. If things kept going as they were—and at no time all summer did they show signs of getting better—I was through as a competitive golfer. I was risking my whole future on a theory which, so far as I knew, nobody but Lew Worsham and I had ever thought about. And who was I—an eighteen-year-old college kid who at the moment couldn't beat his grandmother on the golf course—to say that Lew was right?

It was the kind of crisis that I suppose everybody faces at some time in his life. You have to decide that you want to be a poet even though everybody tells you that poets starve. You have to decide that you're going to be a movie star even though you can't fight your way past the front gate of the studio. You have to decide that you're going to college although your test scores tell you that you'll never make it, or that you're going to walk again although the doctors say you can't.

The summer was agonizing but I stuck to my guns. And all of a sudden everything fell into place. In the Western Pennsylvania Amateur at Oakmont that fall, my shots really started working. In the finals I was paired against Jack Benson, who had won the tournament five times, and I beat him 10 and 8. It was just about the greatest victory of my career up to then, and I knew that I was on my way.

I hope you will remember this story when you yourself get discouraged about golf, as you surely will some day. Every time you adopt something new, it is bound to throw you for a while. It may seem to knock your game to pieces for an entire summer, as it did me when I moved the position of my hands. But if you know that what you are doing is sound, and your pro assures you that it's sound, stick with it. It takes time to mesh any new technique into the rest of your game. It may take weeks or months before you start feeling comfortable and getting results with the grip I described in Chapter 2. When you first start concentrating on holding your head steady, as discussed in Chapter 3, your scores may very well get worse instead of better for a time. But be patient; sooner or later, your day will come. Sometimes it happens overnight, as if by magic.

From 1949, when I shifted to the weak grip, I let my drive alone until 1962. Then I did some more thinking about it. I was getting good distance; I was no longer duck hooking, but I still was dissatisfied with my accuracy off the tee. I was hitting the ball with reasonable consistency, fairly straight; but my shots were going out low and rolling a lot, and the way they would roll was unpredictable. More often than I liked, they were rolling off into the rough.

I wanted very much to win the Masters, which is played on a course where accuracy off the tee is absolutely essential. The fairways are wide at Augusta and there isn't much danger of getting into the rough; you don't have to be much of a golfer to stay in the fairways. But if you want to score there, you have to plan your tee shots as carefully as an architect's drawing; you have to get into a position where you have a good, clear approach to the pin. It's a wonderful course, probably as good a test of golfing skill as can be found anywhere in the world, but I was afraid that I lacked that final sharp edge of skill to cope with it the way I wanted.

So I began analyzing my drive all over again, hoping to find some way of increasing my accuracy. I thought about my own swing and about the theory of the golf swing and, when I was finished, I changed my driving technique in a way that has certainly helped me ever since.

128

The Secret of Accurate Driving

Before I can explain what I did, I'll have to go briefly, just this once, into some of the advanced physics of the golf swing.

You can get a pretty good idea of what the swing is like by holding a plate in your hand, resting it straight up and down on a table, then tilting it to an angle. The rim of the plate will then almost perfectly describe the arc that the clubhead takes, both on the backswing when you get ready to hit, and on the downswing when you do hit. The only difference is that the plate should be flattened a little at the bottom, where it touches the table—for at the bottom of the golf swing, when you get into the hitting area, there is a distance of several inches where a combination of arm action and wrist action makes the clubhead travel in an almost perfectly straight line.

In relation to the ground, the golf swing as seen by a man standing on a glass platform above you shows the clubhead approaching the ball from the inside out—that famous phrase again. Then, for a brief instant, while the clubhead is whipping through the hitting area at its maximum speed, it straightens out. At the moment of impact, the clubhead is traveling—or should be traveling—in the exact same direction as the intended line of flight.

The trick to hitting good iron shots is to make contact with the ball while the clubhead is moving in that straight line, but just before the bottom of the swing. The grooves of the clubface then give it a tremendous backspin which gets the shot quickly into the air and holds it on a straight line. After the impact the clubhead takes a divot, for it is still descending to its lowest point.

Up to 1962, I had been hitting my drives almost like my irons. I teed the ball up no more than a quarter of an inch and made contact with it while the clubhead was still descending. I was hitting the ball just before the bottom of my swing; sometimes I hit the ball and the ground at the same instant. Now I decided: Suppose I tee the ball higher, move it a little further forward, toward my left heel, and, instead of hitting down on it, pick it off the tee with the clubface, at the exact bottom of my swing or perhaps even an instant later? There was nothing new about the idea; many other golfers use it; but I had never before experimented with it.

Theoretically, the new way of teeing the ball would lengthen the distance over which the clubhead was traveling in a straight line—not very much, but perhaps by an inch. And, by adding a little to the

Formerly, I teed the ball low and well back of my left heel when driving.

length of time the clubhead was traveling along the line of flight, I ought to get more accuracy—just as you get more accuracy with a rifle than with a pistol. At the same time, if I teed the ball high enough, I could avoid making any contact at all between clubhead and ground, and eliminate the danger that hitting the ground could dislodge the clubhead from its straight line of motion. I would also get more loft on the ball, cutting down on the roll.

I tried it—I teed up the ball a full inch, higher than any other pro had ever done, to the best of my knowledge—and it worked. Not all at once. Like any other innovation, it took time and practice. I had trouble with it all through the Bing Crosby Tournament and the

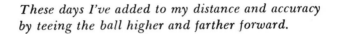

These days I've added to my distance and accuracy by teeing the ball higher and farther forward.

San Diego Open in early 1962. But the new method began to produce results in the San Francisco Open. At Palm Springs it stood up beautifully through a ninety-hole tournament, and I won.

Next we moved to Phoenix, where the tournament alternates each year between the Phoenix Country Club and the Arizona Country Club. I had won it the year before at Arizona, but I had never been able to do very well at the Phoenix Country Club, which has narrow, tree-lined fairways which I had always dreaded. For the first time, now that my new driving method was starting to work, I found myself looking forward eagerly to playing the course. Sure enough, I stayed on the fairways and won the tournament by twelve strokes, the biggest margin of my career in any tournament anywhere. A little later I won the Tournament of Champions at Las Vegas, over a course bordered by heavy rough which had always kept me from winning before, and the National Invitation at Fort Worth, where I had never been in the running before.

By this time I was convinced. Teeing the ball an inch high and in a line with my left heel is now a standard part of my game. There is no question in my mind that this is best of all possible techniques for the drive, providing the maximum possible accuracy and perhaps the maximum distance as well, and I only wish I had started using it years ago. I suggest that you adopt it and stick with it until you have mastered it, for it cannot help but improve your game off the tee.

One word of warning: don't try it when you use a 2-wood or 3-wood off the tee. These clubs are built to be hit down with. To get the most out of them, you have to tee the ball close down against the grass, well back of where you would place it for a drive, and catch it just before the bottom of your swing. When I use the 3-wood, a line drawn through the center of the ball, at right angles to the line of flight, would fall noticeably inside my left heel.

CHAPTER XV

WHAT TO LOOK FOR

AT A TOURNAMENT

As a spectator sport, golf is unique. There is hardly any scenery in America more beautiful than our best golf courses; you can watch a tournament, if you are so minded, for the sheer pleasure of being outdoors and walking around in one of the nation's garden spots. You can go for the enjoyment you get out of watching a group of trained athletes play a game as well as it can possibly be played. Or for the excitement of battle—especially in the final round of a close tournament when three or four or five of the pros, at the top of their game, are charging toward the eighteenth green all with a chance.

Above all, if you yourself are a golfer, you can go to learn. It is a well-known fact that you tend to improve if your golfing companions are better than you are, and tend to get worse if you play frequently with friends who are duffers. Similarly, you can improve your game by watching the tournaments, either in person or on television, for some of the skill of the pros is bound to rub off on you if you're a good observer.

If I were a golf spectator—and sometimes I wish I were so that I could see the whole variegated panorama of the tournaments instead of only my little segment of it—I think I would equip myself with a good pair of binoculars, find the highest point on the course and watch from there, like a forest ranger scanning the entire horizon, all 360 degrees of it. I think this is the way to see the most. I would be sure to have a clear line of vision to several of the tees, a number of the fairways and some of the greens. I would see all the players in the tournament in a great variety of situations.

Or I might seek out one green that sits up fairly high, with a good clear view down the length of the fairway and to the tee. I could sit there, at my ease, and watch how one golfer after another tackles the problems from tee to green. Television coverage of tournaments, done with only a few fixed cameras on the final holes of the course, has proved how much you can see without moving around; if I were feeling lazy, I would emulate the cameras.

Most golfing spectators do it differently. They have a favorite whom they like to follow around, or they follow the player who is leading the tournament. This has its advantages, too, and I'm glad that it's so popular—for, as I have said, I play my best when I have a gallery. The bigger the gallery and the more excited it is, the more I can sense it pulling for me, the better I seem to do. I must have a broad streak of ham in me.

If you follow one threesome around, however, you have to reconcile yourself to missing part of the game, and you also owe it to yourself and to the players to undertake some responsibilities. If the gallery is large, you're going to find it almost impossible to watch both the putting and the tee shots. You'll have to make up your mind which you prefer, heading for the green if you've chosen the putting or for the next tee if you want to see the drives. At least I hope this is what you will do. The attempt to be close up to the green and then rush over to be close up at the tee is nerve-wracking, frustrating for the spectator who tries it and the source of most of the occasional frictions that develop between players and gallery.

The spectator at the green owes it to the players, as a matter of common courtesy, to wait until the last putt is holed out—even if it's a routine 1-footer that a baby could tap in. If you wait only until your favorite in the threesome holes out, then make a dash for the tee, you are going to upset everybody in the threesome, including your favorite, and probably your favorite most of all. Let's suppose you're following Gary Player and he's paired with two young fellows you've hardly heard of. Gary sinks a great 30-footer and, as far as

I usually play my best when I have a gallery, like this one at the Masters in Augusta.

you're concerned, the hole is over. You applaud and rush on while the other two fellows are still trying to line up their putts. If they are young, unknown and struggling to get started on the circuit, they need all the help and courtesy they can get. The noise of the stampede is something they should never have to cope with. They get jittery—and so, now, does Gary. If anything, he suffers more than they do, because he feels that it's all his fault. The next time he putts, he can't help thinking about the mad rush that will follow if he sinks it.

As the crowds at tournaments continue to get larger and larger, I think we're reaching the point where it is best to rope off the entire course—with a big circle at the tee, ropes down the edges of the fairways, and another big circle at the green. I hope that more tournament officials will see fit to do this and that the galleries will cooperate. It helps everybody, golfers and spectators alike. The bigger the circle at tee and green, the more people who can see. And you don't have to be standing at the golfer's elbow to watch his swing; indeed you can get a better view from farther away.

As you watch the tournaments, you will note that no two of the pros are exactly alike. They all have their own little habits, their own little idiosyncrasies, their strengths and sometimes their weaknesses. The more you study them, I am sure, the more you will enjoy the tournaments and the more you will help your own game.

Gary Player's outstanding characteristic is the way he hits and falls back, hits and falls back. He takes such a big swing for such a little man that after he hits the ball he recoils like the barrel of a navy gun. But notice that I said *after*. Watch him closely and you'll see that he's in fine balance when he comes to the ball and that he swings right through it, with all his might. Only after the ball is on its way does he fall back. He's not like the beginner who loses all his power and accuracy by toppling backward before or during the hit.

Note how Gary favors the 4-wood. It's probably the club he likes best. He has great accuracy with it to the greens and often, when the fairways are narrow, even uses it from the tee, sacrificing distance but gaining insurance against trouble. Watch his putting; it's great. And try if you can to find any weakness in his play. It's mighty hard to spot one.

136

You'll note his haberdashery, of course—solid black. He claims that black absorbs the heat of the sun and makes him feel stronger. He doesn't even crack a smile when he says it. But the rest of us pros know better. He's a ham like all of us and he wears the black to attract attention; it's his trade mark. We like to kid him by calling him the best-dressed player in the low-class field.

Jack Nicklaus has that upright swing to distinguish him. Note how high he hits the ball, with every club including the driver; this is the result of his perpendicular swing plus, of course, his immense strength. His drives are sensational but watch him with the long irons; you will see that it is with these clubs, considering their limitations, that he performs his most outstanding feats. Note his peculiar putting stance, with his right foot drawn back in a way that would tie most pros in knots but seems to suit him fine. If he has any weakness at all, at this stage of his career, it is in the sand; you'll see that he doesn't get out of the traps as deftly as some of the other pros. And once in a while, in contrast to his usual accuracy, you'll see one of his drives go badly astray.

Tony Lema has tremendous strength plus a beautiful compact swing, tending toward the upright but certainly not too much so. His swing is so consistent and well controlled that it almost always gives him a good shot, often a great one. He was handicapped in the early years of his career by the fact that he was an in-an-out putter, but in 1964 he suddenly came into his own. He found a putter he liked— matter of fact, I gave it to him—and he proceeded to win four of his next six tournaments. In one of them, the Cleveland Open, he beat me in a playoff. I must say that it's a sort of strange feeling to be beaten by your own putter.

Bobby Nichols is a young fellow who has suddenly developed a tremendous amount of poise; it's amazing how he manages, at such an early stage of his career, to hold his game together when the pressure is on. Take the 1964 P.G.A. tournament. I myself fired four rounds all under 70—the first time this had ever been done in a major tournament. That's about as much pressure as you can apply, yet Nichols stayed right in there and beat me. His greatest asset has been his putting, which out-fantastics the most fantastic putting I ever saw before. It's absolutely amazing how many long ones he drops. And when he doesn't actually drop them, he leaves them so close to the hole that there's no question his second putt will go in as a matter of course.

Ken Venturi is living proof of everything I have said about the power of mind over matter in golf. Back in 1960 he seemed to have the Masters sewed up but lost it. Again in 1961 he was on the verge of winning the Masters, but I birdied the last two holes and beat him. After that Ken's game went to pieces. The fates seemed to be against him; he was thoroughly discouraged, and he suffered the worst collapse ever known for a topflight golfer with a sound swing. But he came right back in 1964 with an entirely new attitude—and won the U.S. Open even though he was close to collapse from the terrific June heat in Washington. This was one of the gamest exhibitions I've ever seen in a tournament. I don't believe Ken has changed anything about his swing or any other part of his game. He certainly hasn't changed anything very much. It was simply a new-found confidence that made him a great player again in '64.

Chi Chi Rodriguez is a man who has turned a handicap into an asset. He is really too small and too light to be a top golfer, but he compensates for his size by his great agility; he manages to get more of his body and his power into his shots than any of us bigger fellows can manage. He's a David who is going to beat a lot of Goliaths in his time, especially if he gives up some of his mannerisms. It's no secret that right now many of us aren't exactly tickled to play in the same threesome with him: his habit of waving his arms to the crowd and throwing his hat over the hole when he sinks a putt can be pretty distracting. I think it distracts him, too, and I've tried to tell him he'd win a lot more money on the tour if he quit showboating.

One of the most consistent money winners over the years is Dow Finsterwald; he doesn't win as many tournaments as he would like to win, but he's almost always somewhere near the top. Watch him and you will see why. He hits the ball left to right, with a slight fade that is easier to control than the hooks that most pros tend to hit. And he's a brainy player, leaning toward the conservative side. Watch how he steers away from trouble on the fairway and aims his approach shots at the fat side of the green. Note his feet-together putting stance, and the old mallet putter he always uses. He has had it for years and he swears by it, on any kind of green. He's certainly deadly with it on his 10- and 12-footers, I'll say that. He hardly ever misses a putt at this distance; he's automatic. Yet, strangely, he usually misses one very short putt a round. It's probably a case of being too fine a putter for his own good. He's so used to dropping those 12-footers that when he finds himself with a real easy putt he can't always take it as seriously as he should.

Doug Ford's outstanding characteristic is the flat swing which I have already mentioned. But what you should really look for in his game is his pitch shots. He has a great variety of them, all of which he executes to perfection. On one hole he will send up a high lob well short of the hole and you will think he has missed the shot, because you expect it to stop dead where it lands. Instead, it rolls right on up to the pin. Next time he hits a low punch shot and you figure he's going way past, but the ball has so much backspin that it grabs and stops as if it had brakes.

Another man to watch around the greens is Jerry Barber, a hard worker who practices as much as anybody in the business, possibly more. He has developed such a deft touch with the putter and pitching clubs that it more than makes up for his lack of power. Notice his extremely upright stance with the putter, and how high on the shaft he holds his hands. And on his pitches and chips, watch him study his lie and the terrain and reach for his club. Whichever iron he chooses, you can be absolutely sure that it is the ideal club for that shot.

For a picture swing, watch Mike Souchak. His swing is so consistent, so beautifully grooved, as to make him a big money winner for many years—even when, as recently, he has had trouble with his putting touch.

To see a drive that is a little out of the ordinary, watch Bill Casper. He hits it left to right but extremely low and hard, and he usually gets a long roll even though you would think the ball had the wrong kind of spin. Note also his putting. This is the part of his game which he practices most; he does it magnificently.

Another player who likes to fade the ball is Bob Rosburg, and he does it with extreme accuracy. I've known how good Bob is since 1947, when he absolutely ran away from me and everybody else in the National Junior Amateur Championship in Los Angeles. Note how fast he plays. He lines up his shots quickly and chooses a club without hesitation; he makes up his mind in a hurry. Even when

It's nice to have the police—the Scottish police—on your side when a well-

wishing gallery at the British Open presses in on you.

putting, he is living proof that you don't have to study the green all day to read it accurately.

Among the young players, take note of Paul Bondeson and the long ball he hits. Also watch Johnny Pott, who always seems on the verge of making it big—and probably will as soon as he learns to put more loft on his drives, which he has been hitting very low up to now and with so much power that they sometimes go astray. There are so many fine young players coming up right now that it would be impossible to discuss them all individually. All I can say is that you will see good, sound, solid and often spectacular golf from youngsters such as Pete Brown, Terry Dill, Raymond Floyd, Frank Beard, Jack Rule, Jr., George Archer, Bert Yancey, Dick Sikes and many others. While watching them you may be looking at a future champion.

Indeed all the players on the pro circuit are well worth watching. If they weren't good, they couldn't make a living. If they weren't dedicated to the game, they couldn't stand the stress, strain and back-breaking work. As I said earlier, in any tournament where there are 150 players, I fear every one of the other 149.

As to what you can learn from watching the pros, I think the chief thing is rhythm; I think you can absorb some of the feeling of easy, fluid motion that all of them have.

If you watch carefully, you will note that about the only two things they have in common are (1) they all hold their heads still—at least they do when they're hitting the ball at their best, and (2) they all are in good balance and squared away at the moment of contact. Aside from this, no two of them swing exactly alike. Their turns are a little different; so is the length of backswing; so is the variation between upright swing and flat. It all goes to prove, I think, the point I tried to impress on you when we were talking about the fundamentals of the game. There are only a few basic rules that you have to follow, and the rest of golf is a matter of doing what comes naturally.

The way the pros swing may vary, but note how seriously they concentrate on every shot, yet how relaxed and natural are their motions. They make the game look easy, don't they? And that's the way it should be. You don't have to twist yourself into a pretzel trying to follow the rules about turn and weight balance that you read in some overly complicated book of instructions. You don't have to beat the ball to death. All you have to do is obey the few basic rules, get comfortable, feel confident—and swing.

There is one other thing I think you can learn from watching the pros, and this is how to get set over the ball. It is partly a matter of stance, and I could have discussed it in Chapter 3 when we focused on the head and feet; it is also partly a matter of starting the swing, so that it could have been mentioned in Chapter 4. I left it out deliberately at that time to avoid confusion—but I think that we should talk about it now.

When I talk about "getting set over the ball," I mean addressing it. As you step up to the ball and get ready to hit, you've got to get your feet into their proper relation to the line of flight. In other words, you've got to take aim with your feet and body. Then, when you put the club behind the ball just before starting your backswing, you've got to take aim with the clubhead, too. And, as you're standing there just before you go to work, you've got to be set solidly and comfortably. You get the feeling, if you do it correctly, that you're right on top of the ball. You don't have to reach for it. You won't have to strain to keep your head steady over it. You have the feeling that if you just take your natural swing, you're bound to hit the ball solidly and send it right where you want it to go. You're set in the way a baseball player gets set in the batter's box, or a basketball player on the foul line.

The moves in getting set are these: First you step up to the ball and get your feet planted. Then you take your grip on the club. You waggle to keep loose, put the clubhead down behind the ball, waggle again and start your backswing.

The waggle is terribly important because you have to keep moving to keep from freezing. There has to be a brief moment when you're more or less standing stock-still, so that you can check your aim and make sure you're in balance. But if that moment lasts too long, your muscles will tense up and you will have a hard time getting the club into motion. You will probably start it back with a jerk instead of the smooth, fluid play of muscles that you want. You may be tempted to pick it up with your wrists, thus violating the cardinal rule of taking it back in one piece. It's the waggle that keeps you from freezing and making these mistakes.

But the wrong kind of waggle can hurt you. If you move your feet while you're waggling, you're going to get out of position. Your aim will be knocked off. Your balance can be affected, also your sense of timing. If you waggle too violently, you can also lose balance. The entire tempo of the swing is set by the way you waggle. A fast, jerky, erratic waggle produces a fast, jerky, erratic swing. Too much waggle tends to speed up the swing and leads to swinging too hard.

The right way to get set over the ball, the right way to waggle, are very hard to describe. They involve delicate little shades of motion, balance and timing. I don't believe anybody could tell you exactly how to do it, either in a book or in person. It's something you have to learn by seeing it done and then developing your own particular method, through practice and trial and error.

So watch this part of tournament play with particular care. You will see a few pros who are dangerously close to being at one of the extremes. Doug Sanders, for example, has a tendency to freeze at times. Gardner Dickinson is another who stands motionless over the ball considerably longer than most of us could manage without getting into trouble. At the opposite end of the scale, Dow Finsterwald sometimes moves his feet while addressing the ball—you can almost see him hop—and when he does this, his aim often goes off.

But most of the pros, you will note, are right in the middle. They manage to get set solidly and still stay loose. Sam Snead in particular has a beautiful way of addressing the ball. He moves just enough to keep from freezing, with an easy, finely timed waggle that gets his backswing started smooth as a milkshake. You can learn a lot by watching how Sam gets set over the ball.

The forward press is something we should talk about for a moment. Most golfers use it and most of the books recommend it. You get set over the ball, finish your waggle and then, before starting the backswing, make a slight move in the opposite direction. You turn the body slightly to the left, moving your arms enough to carry your hands in front of the ball. Your backswing then starts as a sort of recoil action.

If you watch the tournaments, you'll find that almost all the pros use the forward press—except me. I avoid it deliberately. I don't think you need it to get started smoothly, not if you've got a nice loose waggle. And I think it simply adds another motion, a useless one, to your swing. The more motions, the more chance for error, so I don't want any part of it. If you can get along without it, I think you'll be better off, too. But if you're so in the habit of doing it that you would feel lost without it, I certainly wouldn't urge you to change.

CHAPTER XVI

SO LONG–AND
HAPPY GOLFING

A BOOK THIS SIZE doesn't seem very long when you read it. (Not if it's any good—and I hope you haven't found this one a bore.) But when you write a book, it seems very long indeed. It has been months since I first started working on it, years since I first started thinking about it. In a way I have probably been thinking about it most of my life.

Why have I done it? For many reasons, I guess. *Everybody* wants to write a book and see his name on the jacket. Everybody feels he has something important to say. But I did it mostly, I think, because I hoped to convey some of my enthusiasm for golf to you; I'd like to infect the whole world with the golfing virus. And I'd like to see more people playing the game better and enjoying it to the fullest. I'd like to put something back into the game which has given me so much pleasure and earned me such a handsome living.

I started swinging a club, as I mentioned earlier, at the age of four; I was completely hooked on golf by the time I was seven or eight. We had some caddies at the Latrobe Country Club who played a good game, and because I was the pro's son they let me play along. Soon I was beating most of them, despite the age difference, and it was a wonderful feeling. Like all other boys I had been interested in base-

Just about the happiest moment of my golfing career came as the final putt dropped, enabling me to win the 1960 U.S. Open at Cherry Hills.

ball and football, but I gradually pushed these other sports into the background. Somehow I felt that golf was more competitive, had more thrills and satisfactions. I was on my own at golf; I didn't have to depend on anybody else. If I won, it was *my* victory. If I hit a bad shot, I had nobody to blame but myself.

Even in those days, long before I had ever thought of becoming a pro, I hated to hit a bad shot. It pained me; it made me feel awful. That ball was there to be hit *right*. Without constant pressure from my teachers I would never have done my school homework, but nobody had to urge me to do my golfing homework. When something went wrong with my shots, I couldn't wait to get back to the practice tee and go to work.

I began caddying at eleven and eventually became caddymaster at Latrobe. All through the golfing season, I worked on the golf course as a sort of third assistant greens keeper from 7:00 A.M. until noon, had lunch and then worked in the pro shop until 7:00 or 8:00 P.M. My father said I was the worst caddymaster he had ever seen or heard of in his life, because when no one was looking I always locked up the shop and went to the practice tee. I caught a lot of hell from him in those days, but both he and I knew he was secretly on my side. And I don't think I was half so bad as he insisted. I knew how to whip a golf club and do a professional job of shellacking a wood by the time I was fourteen. (And I'm glad I did, for working on my own clubs is now one of my greatest pleasures—and perhaps a competitive asset over the pros who can't do it themselves.)

We had a high school golf team at Latrobe and I could hardly wait to graduate from elementary school and join it. I could beat most of the high school players when I was in the seventh and eighth grades; in my first match on the team, as a freshman in 1943, I shot a 73 and beat a left-hander from the town of Gennett. I've forgotten his name but he gave me almost as big a thrill as winning my first Masters. I would have been the happiest high school freshman in the nation, except that I also tried out for the football team and they told me I was too small even to rate a uniform. Now I'm glad that I didn't make the team because I had more time and energy to devote to golf.

You've heard of vicious circles; mine was a happy circle. The more I played the better I got, and the better I got the more I wanted to play. As a sophomore I was third in the state junior amateur. In 1946 and 1947 I won our district junior amateur and the state amateur, too.

The Junior Amateur of 1947 in Los Angeles was my first national tournament, and none of us could get close to Bob Rosburg. But something happened that was even better than winning. It was there that I first met Bud Worsham. We immediately became great friends and he persuaded me to apply, as he had, for a scholarship at Wake Forest College. The next three and a half years were in many ways the happiest of my life. There were six or seven topnotch players at Wake, and we spent all our spare time playing against one another for dollar Nassaus. It was more than any of us could afford and we played our hearts out.

Then Bud Worsham had his accident and was killed. School was never the same for me. The same scenes and same companions I had once enjoyed so much were suddenly no longer endurable without Bud. I quit school and, without really knowing what I was doing, signed up with the Coast Guard for three years.

For a year I played hardly any golf at all. Then I was transferred to Cleveland and, finding myself in the company of some fellows who had been scratch to 12-handicap shooters in civilian life, I took up the game again. Even when Cleveland was buried under a foot of snow in the winter, we went down to a sheltered part of the lake, to a course called Lake Front, and played to the pins which stood frozen solid in the cups. We played eightsomes, bundled in our winter gear, with a hand warmer inside each heavy mitten and another hand warmer to keep the golf ball from turning into a stone. (We held a reunion in 1961, and one of my proudest possessions is a two dollar bill which all the others autographed for me—in remembrance of the two dollar Nassaus we played over the ice.)

When I got out of the Coast Guard I went back to school. This was the only thing, I realized, that made any sense. But my heart still wasn't in it. I quit again, with one semester to go on my degree, and went back to Cleveland to work as a salesman and try to make something of myself as a golfer on the side.

At the time I still had no real thought of turning pro. Although it's hard to remember now, in these days when the pros earn more than two million dollars a year in tour money alone, and are more than welcome wherever they go, there was a time not so long ago when the golf pro wasn't even admitted to his own clubhouse. I knew some of the disadvantages of the business from listening to my father and I was too proud to live my life as anything like a second-class citizen. So I had some sort of vague hope of becoming a businessman and a top amateur, playing in all the big amateur tournaments.

One of the things that changed my mind, as you may have guessed, was meeting Winnie. It was a case of love at first sight—on my part, at least—but again golf helped smooth the way. Some of my golfing friends lured me into a trip to Pine Valley, the famous New Jersey course, and into a bet where I was to receive one hundred dollars for every stroke I shot under 72 but would have to pay one hundred dollars for every stroke over 80. I had no idea, when I made the agreement, how really tough Pine Valley is. It was a sucker bet, but I was young and in love and nothing could scare me. I had to sink a 30-foot putt on the first hole to get a bogey and my game should have gone to pieces right then and there as I started contemplating how much money I was likely to owe at the end of the day—but I settled down and shot a 68. I won four hundred dollars on my original bet, four hundred dollars more on side bets, and promptly spent most of it on an engagement ring.

In the fall of 1954 I made the big decision. I had won the National Amateur and was supposed to go to England with the Walker Cup team. I wanted to go very badly. I wanted to keep my amateur standing and be a gentleman golfer all my life. But suddenly I realized that I was asking the impossible. I didn't even have enough money to make the trip to England, and I wasn't about to make much more as long as I divided my energies between business and golf. I called Winnie long distance and asked her if she would mind if I skipped the Walker Cup matches and turned pro instead. She didn't hesitate a minute. She said, "I want you to do whatever you want to do." That's the kind of girl she is.

One of my first tournaments as a pro was in Miami. My father and I drove down there together and stayed in the same motel room. We were both full of confidence, but I failed even to make the cut. After the second day of the tournament I was *o-u-t,* OUT. I didn't even go back to the motel room. I ducked my father and went out on the town.

This one of my father and me belongs in the family album.

When I finally got to the room, early in the morning, my father was awake and waiting for me. "What's wrong with you?" he asked. "Are you too lovesick to play?"

I hung my head and said I guessed that I was.

"Well, then marry her," he said. "Get it over with."

151

I got a few hours sleep, put my dad on a plane, and drove nonstop to Winnie's home in Coopersburg, Pa. She was game to marry me then and there, but her parents didn't like the idea and I could hardly blame them. How would you like a daughter to run off with a young fellow who had just turned pro, had thus far failed to earn a nickel at his new job, and who showed up like a wild man badly in need of sleep and a shave?

We couldn't persuade her parents to give their permission, so we had to elope. We went to a justice of the peace in Falls Church, Va., and he asked Winnie if she was twenty-one. She's an honest girl and she was really only twenty, so I kicked her hard to help her say "yes." Perhaps we're not legally married at all. But everything turned out for the best. Once the deed was done, Winnie's parents and I became good friends. I've told you what a great wife Winnie is, and of course you know how happy I am with my career.

I'm not advertising for professionals. As far as I'm concerned, there are too many good ones right now. But if I had had enough money as a youngster to keep my amateur standing, I would have missed some of the greatest experiences a man could ever hope to enjoy.

It's not all a bed of roses, of course. I sometimes think that I would have had a better life had I been born fifty years earlier, when the stakes were not so high and the game was more carefree.

The professionals of the 1920s mostly earned their livings working at some country club; the tour was just a side issue which gave them a chance to break the routine, test their skill and perhaps pick up some extra cash. Even as recently as 1942, a year's total prize money was less than the two hundred thousand dollars now offered for a single tournament. The pros spent most of the year at home; during the tournament season they would go away for a week to play, then return home for a couple of weeks before leaving for another tournament. On the average there were only about thirty-five to forty players to compete for the prize money.

Nowadays the prize money exceeds two million dollars, spread around in no less than forty-five tournaments. The season lasts virtually all year and the pro who wants to take advantage of all the opportunities has to be prepared to travel constantly. Only a few pros have country club jobs. The others have to live off their winnings—and the competition is fierce. Go to any tournament this year and when the last player comes in off the course, as dusk is falling, walk over to the practice tee. You will see more pros there, knocking themselves out to improve their game for the following day, than made up the entire list of competitors in the old days.

Today's golfer has to do something that is quite foreign to the golfer's temperament. He has to keep careful business records and receipts; he has to itemize each day's expense account before he goes to bed; he has to prove where he's been and what he's done to the satisfaction of his own tax man and of Uncle Sam. He has to plan his life far in advance, for you can't just drive into a city where a tournament is being held and expect to find a hotel or motel room five minutes away from the course. Too many golfers make the tour these days, and too many spectators as well, to allow for any hit-or-miss improvising. The pro has to line up his schedule and his living quarters far ahead.

The more successful the golfer, the more the distractions. Believe me, I'm not knocking it. I love the opportunity and security that come from my outside business interests like the Arnold Palmer Company and some other golf and clothing companies. I'm glad that I have to have a lawyer-agent to help plan my career and to write my contracts. I'm delighted that newspapermen like to interview me and that people seek my autograph. But sometimes the outside pressures do get in the way. The 1962 Phoenix Open had to go an extra day, through the Monday, and I couldn't help thinking that a half-dozen important businessmen, directors of the Arnold Palmer Company, were losing the entire day and were waiting impatiently for me to show up at a board meeting in Chattanooga.

The professional golfer can't hope to lead a completely normal life. When our first daughter was expected in 1955, I was about to start the final round of a tournament in Houston when a telephone call came telling me that Winnie had been taken to the hospital. There was nothing much I could do about it, except beg the other players in my threesome to play fast. Then I caught the night plane to Newark, which seemed the fastest way to get home, and waited there at the airport for another plane as the sun was coming up. I could only watch the sunrise and pray that everything was all right, and

The British Open trophy is a great one to win, particularly at a course

like Troon, with hosts so genuinely friendly and pleased by one's success.

then get on another plane which would take me home to find out. I realized, as I walked around in the early morning light, fidgeting and saying my little prayer, that the golfer has a lot of problems which other men are spared. (Everything did turn out all right, of course.)

Still, I sometimes wish that there weren't quite so much pressure on today's successful pro. When I have to start a tournament after posing all morning for photographs that an advertising agency needs for one of the companies in which I have an interest; and some newspapermen have been interviewing me during the breaks; and I get word that my lawyer has been trying to get hold of me on the phone; and there's a wire at the golf course asking me to take part in a charity television show—when all these things happen, as they so often do, I sometimes long for the good old days when nobody knew me from Adam and all I had to do was practice and play golf, practice and play golf, without any distractions at all.

But then I get a few days' break between tournaments and I step into my airplane and fly home, something that I couldn't have done until I became successful at golf, something that none of yesterday's pros could afford to do. It's a plane that golf bought me, and it takes me to a home that golf bought me, and to a family which would never have had its present comforts and opportunities without golf. True, the house is already obsolete. After I built it, I found I had to add an extra room to serve as an office; now the office is getting too small to hold all of the filing cabinets I need and the secretary who helps me answer my mail. I'll surely have to move into a bigger place one of these days. Still, it's a house I love and I never would have had it without golf.

I think about all the wonderful things that have happened to me. I think how as a small-town boy I used to marvel at the movie stars who, according to rumor, made such miraculous sums as a hundred dollars a week. I think how I used to stare star-struck at Bob Hope and marvel that Bob Hope is now a friend of mine: I remember the day I helped him win the pro-am at Phoenix in 1963 and how he spent the entire evening calling all his friends around the nation to brag about it. I think about making a movie with him in England in the summer of 1962, *Call Me Bwana*, becoming something of a movie star myself. Not a star, really, not even a halfway decent actor—just a small-town boy who, thanks to golf, had an opportunity he would never have dreamed of. It occurs to me that if I were ever in serious trouble and needed a friend's helping hand, Bob Hope would probably want me to call him.

I think about the other celebrities I have met and played golf with: Bing Crosby, Mickey Rooney, James Garner, Phil Harris. Wonderful fellows, all of them great people to know. I think about playing golf with Dwight D. Eisenhower, while he was President of the United States and since. That's another fabulous thing about golf. It brings all men together within the firm bonds of a strong mutual interest: golfers are automatically friends. I can feel comfortable and take intense pleasure playing golf with a President—or with a young fellow who supports himself as a busboy.

I think about the trips I have taken: to South Africa to play a series of exhibitions with my good friend Gary Player, to Canada, England, Scotland, Ireland, Wales, France, Greece, Italy, Japan Hong Kong, the Philippines, Australia, Rhodesia, the Belgian Congo, Mexico, Argentina, Panama and Colombia. Golf is already one of the most international of all sports. Some day it may be *the* international sport, the international language which will draw all men of all nations together in friendship.

These are the high spots of my career—but I've even enjoyed the low spots. I have a great affection for the old secondhand trailer, surely on some junkheap by now, in which Winnie and I first made the tour. I love the memory of the secondhand trailer we owned (thanks to a six hundred dollar loan from her father) which had three rooms and bath and was wonderfully comfortable, but was too heavy for my automobile to pull. I remember how we had to drive all night to a tournament at Palm Beach, finally arriving at 5:00 A.M., and how I teed off at 8:00 A.M. and shot an 85. I recall how on the trip back home we came to an icy hill which we couldn't make under our own power, and how Winnie got out to push. I remember the bursitis that struck me my first year on the tour and made me fearful that I would never be able to play again—a Dr. Needles, in St. Petersburg, gave me a shot of cortisone that cured it forever. (Or maybe I just thought it was cortisone. Perhaps my ailment was strictly in my head and Dr. Needles was a wise psychologist who injected me with salt solution and confidence.)

I've been up and I've been down, and either way I've enjoyed every minute of it. I'm grateful to the galleries who follow me around and I always try to play my best for them; when I fail, it hurts me more than it disappoints them. I like to sign autographs. I guess I just plain like people.

I hope this book has helped you play better golf. I feel confident that it has—or will. But mostly I hope it helps you enjoy the game more, as player or as spectator. I'm in love with golf and I want everybody else to share my love affair.

ACKNOWLEDGMENTS

My sincere thanks are extended to Ernest Havemann for the invaluable assistance he gave me in collecting and organizing the material for this book.

I am also grateful to the magazine *Sports Illustrated,* in which much of the material in this book appeared originally in abbreviated form. Its editors cooperated most helpfully in the preparation both of the magazine articles and the expanded book version.

Peter Schwed, of Simon and Schuster, is the one who directed the preparation of the book itself, and I appreciate his editorial advice.

All the line drawings in the book are the work of Francis Golden, and his contribution to my book is a most meaningful one.

Acknowledgments are also in order to the photographers named below, who kindly gave consent for the inclusion of their work, as well as to *Sports Illustrated,* which commissioned all the photographs except those appearing on pages 65 and 151:

James Drake—page 123
Golf Digest—page 151
Clyde Hare—page 11
Art Kane—front and back endpapers
Richard Meek—page 2, the color pages following page 16 and
    page 32, pages 68–69, 117
P. A. Reuter Photos Ltd.—page 65
Art Rickerby—pages 106–107, 135
Brian Seed—pages 47, 79, 98–99, 140–141, 154–155
John Zimmerman—pages 58–59, 121, 147

—ARNOLD PALMER

12